Ike Ijeh

# Designing London

## Understanding the character of the city

LUND
HUMPHRIES

First published in 2020 by Lund Humphries

Lund Humphries
Office 3, Book House
261A City Road
London EC1V 1JX
UK

www.lundhumphries.com

ISBN: 978–1–84822–326–4

A Cataloguing-in-Publication record for this book is
available from the British Library.

Front cover: The dome of St Paul's Cathedral viewed
from One New Change.
Photo: Ike Ijeh.

Copyedited by Julie Gunz
Designed by Jacqui Cornish
Set in Circular Std
Printed in Slovakia

# Contents

Acknowledgements   5

Introduction   6

**PART I: DEFINING LONDON'S URBAN CHARACTER**   9

**Human Capital: Understanding London's Character**   11
     Villages   11
     Diversity and Contrast   13
     Unplanned Development   13
     Public vs Private   16
     Democracy   18
     Domesticity   18
     Nature   20
     Informality and Irregularity   22
     Humanity   23

**London Falling: The Collapse of London's Character**   25
     Tall Buildings   25
     Conservation   27
     Housing Crisis   29
     Design   31
     Public Space   32

**A Tale of Five Cities: Comparative Urban Set-Pieces**   34
     London vs Berlin   34
     London vs New York   36
     London vs Paris   38
     London vs Rome   40

**PART II: PROTECTING LONDON'S URBAN CHARACTER**   43

     Alleyways   45
     Art   46
     Climate   47
     Colour   49
     Density   51
     Entrances   53
     Fountains   55
     Furniture   57

Grain  58
Grid  61
Height  63
Housing  66
Lighting  69
Materials  70
Names  73
Paving  75
Planning  76
Signage  79
Squares  81
Streets  88
Style  98
Topography  101
Transport  103
Trees  104
Uses  105
Views  111
Waterways  113


**PART III: ENHANCING LONDON'S URBAN CHARACTER**  117

**Projects that Harm London's Urban Character**  119

5 Broadgate  119
20 Fenchurch Street  121
22 Bishopsgate  123
Chapter Spitalfields  125
ME London Hotel  127
Nine Elms  129
Nova Victoria  131
One New Change  133

**Projects that Enhance London's Urban Character**  135

60 Queen Victoria Street  135
Chichester Rents  137
Eccleston Yards  139
King's Cross Central  141
McGrath Road  143
Newport Street Gallery  146
One Cartwright Gardens  147
The Shard  149


Appendix  152
Notes  156
Index  157
Illustration Credits  160

# Acknowledgements

*This book is dedicated to my family, especially my loving and irreplaceable wife, my loyal and supportive parents, my brave and beautiful sisters and my precious baby son.*

First and foremost, I would like to thank my commissioning editor Val Rose for encouraging me to write this book. Without her patience, understanding, advice and support this book would simply not have been possible. I would also like to thank Jacqui Cornish, Sarah Thorowgood, Pam Bertram and Julie Gunz for their diligent work in the production stages of this book. Further thanks go to the following architectural practices for their generosity in granting permission for the use of a selection of their photographs in this book: BuckleyGrayYeoman, Caruso St John, Maccreanor Lavington, ORMS and Stanton Williams. For this same reason I would like to extend thanks to Argent Property Development Services and Sam Lopez and Benno Rembeck for helping to secure the photographs. I would also like to thank Professor Tony Travers of the London School of Economics – a man who knows London better than most – who was kind enough to read excerpts of this book in their very earliest form and offer encouragement and advice. I would like to thank my father for taking me to the top of the campanile at Westminster Cathedral as a little boy and helping kick-start my love affair with London and architecture. I would like to extend my warmest thanks and gratitude to my patient and understanding wife who tolerated this book as a third member of our new marriage both before and after the birth of our first child. And, last but not least, I would like to thank my beloved city of London, of whom I continue to discover new things and which continues to fascinate, inspire and amaze me every day.

# Introduction

London is dying. Not, of course, in any literal sense. The city remains the largest in Western Europe and one of the wealthiest capitals in the world. It alternately shares the title of world's leading financial centre with New York City and creates almost a quarter of the UK's entire GDP. London remains the only city in the world to have hosted three modern summer Olympic Games and boasts the largest concentration of universities in Europe. The city is undoubtedly one of the world's foremost cultural capitals and for most of the past two decades has either been the first or second most visited city in the world. Equally, with 8.8 million inhabitants and rising, London has surpassed its previous 1939 peak and its population is the highest it has ever been. Furthermore, with over 300 languages spoken, it is one of the most diverse cities on earth.

Clearly, London's architecture and built environment plays a significant role in the city's success and reputation. Boasting more UNESCO World Heritage Sites than Paris, Lisbon and Edinburgh combined, the English capital hosts some of the world's most famous urban landmarks and offers an exhilarating mix of ancient and modern architecture. Much of that architecture has helped form an indelible image of the city's urban character for millions in London, Britain and around the world. But now, perhaps more than at any other time in London's recent history, that character is under threat.

London finds itself in the grip of a period of unprecedented urban change. Some of the highest city land values in the world have helped fuel a building boom that is dramatically changing the physical form of the city. Change is by no means a stranger to London and, perhaps more than any other world city, London's long history shows an extraordinary ability to adapt and evolve as the ravages of war, fire, flooding, cultural upheavals and financial crashes periodically

demand. But the change we witness today is different and across the city there is evidence of a new generation of inept and insensitive architecture that is actively damaging London's urban character. Spiralling house prices have intensified the pressure for development, leading to a spate of high-rise, high-end schemes that are completely superfluous to London's housing need. At the same time, a shortage of affordable housing has sparked a housing crisis, one whose impact has been rendered all the more damaging by an over-provision of unaffordable housing and by the generally poor standard of design. While there are moments of real quality within the residential sector, much of it is a reductive exercise in floorplate duplication, leading to repetitious slabs of dense housing whose crushing banality suppresses the famous individuality of London's various neighbourhoods.

Nowhere is this trend more pernicious than within the area of tall buildings. In a traditionally low-rise city, hundreds of towers have either been constructed or are proposed, many controversially located in the city's most historic areas or lining its greatest public landmark, the River Thames (Fig.1). Iconic heritage assets are continually under threat – if not from demolition then from severe overshadowing from nearby developments. It is now common practice to hijack 'regeneration' as justification for all manner of inappropriate design, with social impoverishment blithely replaced by architectural blight. And time and time again, planning policy is either too weak to form an effective check and balance – as in the case of the infamous Walkie Talkie tower at 20 Fenchurch Street – or is deliberately ignored.

But underlying all these sad instances is something much worse. It is a fundamental failure among the design and development communities to understand the unique character of London. First and foremost, this involves a failure to recognise

1    The rapid expansion of tall buildings in the City of London, the capital's oldest district, has been one of the most conspicuous and controversial signs of the undermining of London's character over the past two decades.

the importance of context, not for its erroneously perceived restrictive limitations, but for the opportunities it presents to respond to London's development challenges with design solutions that enhance its special character rather than undermine it. All too often, this involves a failure to cherish the genial tenets of urbanism that have been the seeds of London's success; qualities such as scale, proportion, materials, informality and intimacy. This series of chronic negations is slowly but surely chipping away at the unique and precious character that is central to London's identity as a city and that renders the capital such an attractive location for development in the first place. In other words, the golden eggs are poisoning the goose. Increasingly in London we see the same incongruous, identikit brand of globalised architectural anonymity that dilutes the character and individuality that makes cities everywhere, especially chaotic, kaleidoscopic London, unique.

The irony is that in today's planning and architecture environment, urban character is supposedly all the rage. It is frequently cited by planners, developers and architects as something they wish to protect and enhance, and its ubiquitous 'placemaking' doppelgänger now dominates professional planning and architectural parlance. But little or no effort is ever made to define urban character in specific or quantitative terms. On one level this is understandable. Urban character is not a distinct or scientific entity; it cannot be described in definitive historic or decorative terms like an architectural style, nor does it have measurable technical or structural attributes like a building or a bridge. Part of the quality and charm of urban character is its very amorphous and even atmospheric nature; the 'feeling' of a place is always harder to describe than its 'look'. But that 'feeling' is an absolutely integral part of how we judge and experience cities. Yet, how that 'feeling' is constructed is rarely understood. The problem with something that is difficult to understand is that it is easy to ignore. And that is exactly the crisis London is currently facing today.

It is a crisis which this book will seek to directly address. It will attempt to definitively and prescriptively define, perhaps for the first time, what London's urban character is and the various physical, social and environmental elements of which it is composed. It will then seek to highlight specific design and spatial strategies by which that character can be protected. And finally, by listing case studies of recent London developments that form examples of where that character has either been improved or undermined, it will seek to provide quantifiable evidence of where and how London's urban character can be enhanced.

Throughout, this book will strive to forge a deeper understanding of London's urban character so that those charged with developing the city will be better equipped to intervene in a manner that strengthens rather than weakens the city's unique identity. This is no manifesto to suppress change, but a strategy to enrich it.

Urban character is important to all cities, but it is especially so to London. London is sprawling, chaotic, ravenous, lazy, grand, casual, greedy, proud, restless, competitive, clever, stubborn, slow, cold, warm, detached, imperious – full of all the wry contradictions and pompous little vanities we find in each and every one of us. Accordingly, it is the most human of cities: it is what writer Peter Ackroyd described as 'a living, breathing organism, with its own laws of growth and change'.[1] The architectural expression of those laws once compelled seminal Danish urbanist Steen Eiler Rasmussen to describe London as 'one of the most civilised cities on earth'.[2] Reviving the intoxicating richness, colour, energy and dynamism of London's urban character is the key to ensuring that that precious civility survives.

# Part I
# Defining London's Urban Character

2   People walk through Jean Nouvel's One New
Change (2010), a new retail, leisure and office
development behind St Paul's Cathedral (1710).

# Human Capital: Understanding London's Character

How does one define the character of a city? Can we assess it in the way we assess human personality? Can a city be kind? Can it be selfish? Can it be wise? Can it be cruel? And if we do decide that cities can be assessed in this way, what is London's character and what makes it different to Adelaide, Berlin, Kolkata or Denver? Paris is known as the 'City of Lights' because of its illuminated monuments, its early municipal adoption of street lighting and, more obliquely, because of its intellectual role during the Age of Enlightenment. These are all elements which inform popular perceptions of the city's luminous character to this day. New York is allegedly known as the 'Big Apple' because of midwestern resentment of the city's perceived greed in consuming a disproportionate bite of American wealth, energy and culture. Few New Yorkers would argue with this aggrieved depiction of a city character seared with rapacious vigour. Rome is called the 'Eternal City' for obvious reasons relating to its antiquity and age. And London's most popular colloquial epithet is the 'Big Smoke', an unflattering reference to the appalling pollution the city endured throughout much of the 19th and the first half of the 20th centuries. But do these glib, titular labels really give us anything more than a superficial snapshot of what really makes a city tick? If we concede there is more to London than pollution, then what constitutes the 'more'?

## VILLAGES

In order to define and understand London's character, we must first look at how the city developed. London was founded by the Romans 2000 years ago in the area where the City of London stands today. This is the oldest part of the capital and by and large constitutes its geographical centre. But it is important to note that London did not expand in a steady, radial, concentric fashion to occupy the 610 square miles it measures today. It was a choppy and uneven accumulation of neighbouring towns and villages in a messy process dragged out over several centuries.

After the City itself, first to be consumed was Westminster, its marshy, Thorney Island core eventually transformed into London's seat of monarchy, church and state, a twin focal point for the City which endured as the seat of commerce. Next, London snaked along Ludgate Hill and Aldwych to fill the gap between its eastern and western extremities, merging the City and Westminster together beyond the City's ancient walls. It was not until the 17th and 18th centuries that London was to spread meaningfully again, establishing new districts in Covent Garden, Bloomsbury and Mayfair. But it was the 19th century when London's expansion, turbocharged by the Industrial Revolution, exploded beyond all previous measure. Outlying westerly districts like Kensington and Chelsea were gobbled up and London spread south of the River Thames for the first time, consuming the neighbouring town of Southwark. This period also saw the origins of suburbanisation in London, with the outlying villages of Islington, Hackney, Finsbury, Lambeth, Shoreditch and Camden all coming under London's irresistible orbit. The 20th century saw London grow again, sucking up towns even further afield such as Greenwich, Woolwich, Sydenham, Lewisham, Finchley, Walthamstow, Wembley, Wood Green and Ealing, and effectively repurposing each acquisition from satellite to suburb. The long process of geographic growth was only halted in 1965 with the creation of Greater London and the establishment of the green

3   Cafe culture in Seymour Place, Marylebone: despite London's scale, it provides a concentration of distinct 'village' neighbourhoods, each with their own unique charm and character.

belt to check London's sprawl. This is when we first saw the city boundaries that still apply today.

The point to this process is that there is not one London, but several. The city is often called a collection of villages and the term is both physically and figuratively accurate (Fig.3). London was never planned as a single entity, it colonised and combined multiple settlements into one varied and gigantic whole like a vast urbanised rendition of a split personality. This has had a unique impact on the city's character. London offers astonishing levels of diversity between its different districts and each one has a special identity very often unique to itself. Kensington is associated with royalty and culture, Bloomsbury resounds with academia, Camden is home to alternative culture, Spitalfields is famous for its markets, Kew for its gardens and Hampstead for its heath and intellectuals. Of course, every city will have different characteristics to each constituent part. But in London these are more deeply ingrained because the pattern of the city's development often meant that each neighbourhood had its own independent identity before it was swallowed up. And even after their integration into the capital these independent identities remained, so much so that rather than having one character, London has several parallel characters operating at the same time. Therefore, understanding and respecting the unique and divergent quality of London's village composition is crucial to understanding the overall character of the city.

## DIVERSITY AND CONTRAST

And what, then, of this overall character? A city cannot merely be a sum of its parts or else it ceases to be a city; it must have thematic consistencies that define it as a single civic entity unique from other single civic entities, as the popular epithets at the start of this chapter showed. Consequently, two of London's strongest characteristics stem from its very village composition, diversity and contrast. London is a resolutely diverse city and its village make-up establishes a pattern of diversity that extends into multiple areas of the capital's urban fabric. This includes a diversity of architectural styles, materials, colours, street and public space typologies, building forms and soft and hard landscaping treatments. This ingrained lack of uniformity therefore, is also a unique aspect of London's wider character.

With diversity inevitably comes contrast, and contrast too forms a major theme of London's urban character. All manner of visual and social contrasts can be found operating within the capital's urban fabric: rich and poor, new and old, high-rise and low-rise, city and park, formal and informal, regular and irregular, public and private, intimate and open, steel and stone (Fig.4). The Inns of Court encapsulate these principles well, Georgian one minute, Elizabethan the next, monumental one minute, intimate the next, expansive lawns one minute, miniaturised courtyards and passageways the next and so on.

Again, to a degree, all cities will include any number of these juxtapositions as part of their urban DNA. But London's more pronounced reliance on diversity and predominant rejection of uniformity ensures that the city embraces contrast as one of its most powerful characteristic themes. And herein lies one of the problems for London's character as discussed in the following chapter. Contrast can be cynically exploited as justification for virtually any kind of development. If a city has a tradition of contrast then it surely does not matter if, for instance, a 60-storey tower is placed beside a Grade I-listed Gothic church, particularly if the planning system is vague and imprecise enough not explicitly to prohibit such a course of action. While contrast can obviously be an effective tool in breeding a dynamic and invigorating cityscape full of unexpected drama and tension – as is often the case in London – it is important not to misconstrue contrast as chaos by manipulating it as a precursor to the kind of inappropriate development that can harm character. The aforesaid planning system should be the statutory arbiter that prevents this from happening but, as we shall see, this is not always the case in London (Fig.5).

## UNPLANNED DEVELOPMENT

London has always been an unplanned city. In its long history only one successful grand urban plan was imposed on the city, that of George IV and John Nash's Via Triumphalis which established much of the layout and character of central London we see to this day (Fig.6). Other grand city-wide schemes, such as Charles II and Sir Christopher Wren's plans to rebuild London as a great, axial baroque city after the Great Fire of London, inevitably fell by the wayside. Historically, London has grown, and continues to grow, by instinct rather than intent, ruthlessly galvanised by a raw and guttural imperative that demands continuity yet embraces change. This may help explain why London has never been a planned city in the manner of other European capitals such as Paris or Vienna or even Washington DC. Uniquely in Europe and in spite of its overtly imperial past, the historical development of the streets, public spaces and buildings that form London's urban character has assumed an erratic and stubbornly haphazard form that owes relatively little to the autocratic directives of kings, barons or emperors and has much more to do with London's tradition of loose and organic planning.

Of course, London does have a planning system. And in many ways, that planning system is intensely onerous and prescriptive, as anyone who has tried to build a house extension or erect an advertising hoarding will painfully attest. Equally, London's municipal heritage should be a source of great pride and in the LCC (London County Council) of 1889 to 1965, successor to the almost as successful Metropolitan Board of Works of 1855, London had the first dedicated metropolitan

4    Throgmorton Street, City of London: London's
dynamic mix of old and new helps ensures that
diversity is hardwired into its character.

5    The view from Greenwich Park of the Old Royal Naval College (1669) and the towers of Canary Wharf is typical of the stark manner in which contrast is often handled in the city.

6    John Nash and George IV's ambitious Via Triumphalis of the 1820s culminates in the formal Waterloo Place and is the only major historic example of the successful implementation of a grand plan for the city.

7 Though recent years have seen a massive increase in the construction of tall buildings in the capital, the lack of an overall skyscraper policy is indicative of the city's empirical approach to planning.

government in the world and benefited from waves of programmes of social, housing and infrastructure improvements. But at a strategic level, London's planning system is fractured and contradictory, with each of London's 33 boroughs able to set their own planning agendas with no mandatory recourse to each other or the city as a whole. Today, the Greater London Assembly attempts to provide a strategic political overview but has limited powers and offers aspirational rather than prescriptive guidelines. For instance, among historic capital cities London is unique in having no city-wide tall buildings policy and the London Plan (the mayor's official development strategy for the city) merely calls for tall buildings to 'enhance the skyline', an indeterminate platitude open to all manner of abuse and misinterpretation (Fig.7).

Historically, this tradition of informal planning has had a clear impact on London's urban character and continues to do so to this day. The relative lack of strategic specificity and prescription certainly gives London dynamic flexibility to respond to all manner of demographic or economic events, as witnessed by the regeneration of Canary Wharf in the 1980s and the gentrification and creeping

commercialisation of much of the East End since the late 1990s. But it also leaves London's heritage and identity potentially exposed to harmful corrosion and makes it harder to enforce coherent, coordinated visions for the city's improvement. The canny inscription carved on the Monument in 1677 is just as applicable today as it was 350 years ago: 'Haste is seen everywhere, London rises again, whether with greater speed or greater magnificence is doubtful, three short years complete that which was considered the work of an age'.

## PUBLIC VS PRIVATE

London's historic lack of political authoritarianism and, as we have seen, its relaxed approach to formal public sector planning have left London's development, and character, disproportionately exposed to private sector influence, certainly in comparison to other European cities. This tradition of private development therefore plays an enormous role in London's urban character. Perhaps its most obvious manifestation is the London square, essentially a residential reinterpretation of continental equivalents assembled, in this instance, by means of private speculation rather than public subsidy. Squares are an emblematic part of central London's urban character but, with well over three-quarters of them the result of private speculation, there are key differences between how they are presented in London and generally on the continent. In Europe, public space was frequently conspicuously manipulated as a device for civic display or political strategy. As the Anglophile Danish architect and writer Steen Eiler Rasmussen observed, a French, German or Russian square would often feature an emotional baroque climax, such as a statue or monument as its centrepiece. He identified a typical English square, however, as 'merely a place where people of the same class had their houses'.[3]

Another manifestation of private development that had a significant impact on London's character are the Great Estates of central London, significant tracts of land originally developed by various aristocratic interests, usually for commercial speculation. Again, as with London's village composition, each estate assumes unique characteristics that bestow their own individual identities. The Cadogan Estate, for instance, is synonymous with blood-red brick buildings and terracotta facades, whereas the genteel neoclassicism of the Bedford Estate lends it an air of scholarly repose. Equally, while the Baron Haussmanns of Europe could flatten whole neighbourhoods when they wished to create a grand square or monumental boulevard, the strength and intransigence of London's private ownership traditions made this impossible. Therefore, in London, we often see formal thoroughfares squeezed along the boundaries between neighbouring estates, such as at Kingsway or the Mall.

This more pragmatic approach represents broader Anglo-Saxon suspicions about the untrammelled incursion of the public sector. In 17th-century Paris, and without a hint of irony, the Sun King Louis XIV could declare 'l'état, c'est moi' ('I am the state'). In the 1980s, President François Mitterrand continued the French tradition of state-sponsored 'gloire' with his grands projets. So irked was style guru Sir Terence Conran about the civic one-upmanship that Paris was gaining over London at the time that he allegedly asked Prime Minister Margaret Thatcher whether a similar

programme could not be undertaken here. Perhaps apocryphally, perhaps not, she is said to have replied by offering him the commission to redesign the Cabinet office table.

Another possible civic symptom of Margaret Thatcher's evident disdain for municipal largesse is the emergence of the privately-owned public space London, increasingly noted in recent years. Places like Paternoster Square and every single public space in Canary Wharf, for instance, exude the impression and convention of being public spaces, but they are in fact privately owned. In recent years this has become a contentious arrangement which some have criticised as the privatisation of public space and, on the face of it, this would initially appear to be a fair accusation. But is the nature of public space, and thereby the impact it has on public life, determined by ownership alone? It is likely that a whole raft of other influences are more pertinent than ownership itself; management, accessibility, social conditions and security are far more likely to have a direct impact on the nature of a place than whether or not it is publicly owned. So privately-owned public spaces are nothing new to London and, if designed and managed well, can make as successful a contribution to public life and urban character as their state or council-owned equivalents (Fig.8). Parliament Square, for example,

8   Though controversial for some, the recent expansion of private public spaces such as More London (2003) is a continuation of historic trends in the capital.

is entirely in public ownership and is managed by both the City of Westminster and Transport for London. And yet, it presents one of the most poorly designed, inhospitable and inaccessible urban environments of any major public space in the city.

## DEMOCRACY

With the state effectively stepping back as the primary provider of public space in London during much of the city's development, the vacuum was eventually filled with a new idea that came to form a key part of the city's urban character and public realm: democracy. The rights and privileges of the individual were asserted in perhaps their earliest form (within an urban context at least) in London. Here, the capital's perennial disposition towards volatile and unregulated development conspired to afford the individual gentleman, builder, speculator or rogue, as much or even greater power to influence the built form of his city as the king or the state, as the frustration of Wren's post-Great Fire of London reconstruction plans proved.

As a French visitor to St James's Park disparagingly but incisively observed shortly after

Charles II had ordered the gates of the former royal gardens thrown open to the public in 1669 and effectively established today's royal parks, 'It is a strange sight . . . to see the flower of the nobility and the first ladies of the Court mingling in confusion with the vilest populace. Such is the taste of the English: it is part of what they call their liberty'[4] (Fig.9). We also see democratic egalitarianism practised in many forms within London's built environment. Its stellar heritage of early and mid-20th century social housing, the socially and economically mixed demography of many of its neighbourhoods, the pioneering municipal legacy of the LCC and the aforesaid opening of the royal parks to the public are all indicative of a city with a pluralist, progressive and socially inclusive urban character.

## DOMESTICITY

One of the strongest elements of London's urban character is the residential nature of the city. Clearly all cities have residents. But in London, the residential character persists in all areas of the city and not just those committed to housing.

9　Regent's Park: Charles II's transfer of royal hunting grounds to public ownership in the 1660s created some of the world's first public parks and was emblematic of the manner in which London's public realm incorporates democratic ideals.

10   Barton Street, Westminster (1722): the ubiquity of the London terraced street reflects the huge extent to which domesticity is embedded into the city's character.

Consequently, European-style civic squares are adapted to become residential garden squares, residential garden squares are retrofitted for commercial use (i.e. Soho, Golden and Leicester Squares), public parks become enlarged civic adaptations of private amenity space and the residential terrace becomes a ubiquitous, multifunctional and highly versatile townscape template containing all manner of uses from shops to universities. In so doing, London's residential character becomes almost indivisible from its civic identity (Fig.10).

London's residential character is not just a story of private squares and terraces, but of pioneering social housing too. Today, 24 per cent of London housing is social housing[5] and historically it has made an enormous contribution to the city's character. The Boundary Estate was created on the boundary of Tower Hamlets and Hackney in

1899 and today ranks as the world's oldest council estate. It was pioneering in architectural as well as social terms and much of the estate is now Grade II-listed. Containing a series of handsome, gabled brick mansion blocks arranged around wide avenues emanating from a planted ornamental circus, the development applied the elegant urban conventions of the West End to help elevate the then appalling social conditions of the East End. The extraordinary result emphasised the extent to which public benevolence was once an intrinsic part of London's municipal administration and the scheme contributed significantly to London's early 20th-century reputation for humane metropolitan civility.

This reputation was further enhanced by subsequent generations of exceptional social housing works. The Peabody and Guinness Trusts spearheaded public housing across the city and their distinctive respective yellow- and red-brick flat blocks became a familiar sight within the capital's urban fabric, as they are still today. Later, the works of architects like Berthold Lubetkin and Neave Brown modernised this tradition, with the latter's extraordinary Alexandra Road Estate dramatically reinterpreting London's terrace typology in operatic, brutalist form. All these projects brought the highest standards of design to those on the lowest incomes in order to gently recalibrate London's traditional terraced housing into a style that placed more emphasis on communality, connectivity and inclusion, elements that strongly permeate the character of London's social housing today.

Bound within both private and public models of domesticity is a sense of intimacy and enclosure that is also a key part of London's character. London terraces are sometimes huddled around narrow lanes and many of its early housing estates are clustered around sheltered courtyards that offer moments of tranquillity and repose that help soften the urban condition. It is these kinds of spatial and architectural solutions, such as the human scale of the terrace house and the domestic emphasis on intimacy and landscaping, that enable London to accommodate almost nine million people in mass housing solutions that address, rather than alienate, the individual.

## NATURE

This process of softening or humanising the urban condition is a constant preoccupation of London's urban character and, as well as the city's housing, there is another important element harnessed to channel it: nature. London is one of the greenest big cities in the world, with more than a third of its area allocated to public parks and gardens. But the ingrained naturalistic allegiances of London's urban character are not solely conveyed through the quantity of green spaces in the capital; the idyll of natural landscape is burned deep into London's civic consciousness and urban fabric. It is not by accident that London's oldest square is referred to as a garden (Covent Garden) and its largest square referred to as fields (Lincoln's Inn Fields). These are symptoms of a deep psychological affinity with the natural world that has endured for centuries and survived, despite the fact that it was this most green of cities that created the world's first modern megalopolis in its rampant industrial expansion during the 19th century.

The origins of London's natural affinities probably lie in a long-established national veneration of the English countryside as an idealised residential retreat. This is a cultural aspiration that found architectural voice in the

11   Buckingham Palace submerged in the lush greenery of St James's Park is evidence of how much of London's civic and urban aspect is framed by natural landscape.

12 The Foreign Office (1860), front view. The contrast between the formal front and informal rear of the Foreign Office shows how good London architecture can respond to both urban and natural contexts.

13 The Foreign Office (1860), rear view.

picturesque and romantic movements of the late 18th and early 19th centuries, a movement whose squares, thoroughfares and terraces were critical in establishing the character of central London and the West End as we see them today. This has led to London's character assuming a hybrid form, unique in Europe, that sees its urban fabric repeatedly set against a natural counterfoil. The great architectural historian Nikolaus Pevsner observed that Buckingham Palace 'is surely the only royal palace in any major capital which has its lawns and lake and faces a park'.[6] As the great urban climax

of royal power, it is indeed virtually impossible to imagine Buckingham Palace not surrounded by cafes and shops and served by a metro station were it located in Barcelona or Budapest. But in London it is utterly submerged in blankets of rolling greenery that almost give it the impression of a colossal country mansion rather than that of an iconic, cosmopolitan landmark (Fig.11).

London's strong parkland context is also capable of having a direct impact on its architecture. At Giles Gilbert Scott's 1860s Foreign Office, as one might expect, the building presents a formal, palatial and monumental frontage to Whitehall, with Edwin Lutyens ensuring that the Cenotaph was centred on its grand facade 60 years later (Fig.12). But by the time the rear facade overlooking St James's Park is reached, the formality has dissolved entirely into a quaint, asymmetrical dreamscape of curved bays and turreted towers, all conceived as an irrepressibly romantic response to the lush, picturesque landscape of the park opposite (Fig.13). Between these two opposing facades lies the paradox of London: the city's best architecture must be nimble and nuanced enough to forge an urban response that is equally comfortable within a natural context.

In a similar way, this hybrid natural/urban state is also evident in another key ingredient of the city's character, the square. With their lush central gardens overlooked by residential terraces, they not only provide a seamless synthesis of nature and urbanity, but they also form a more organic version of the European civic square. Ultimately, they prove how, in London, it is often the buildings that are configured as the urban backdrop rather than nature, a picturesque and humanistic reversal of the conventional civic priorities found in scores of cities across the world.

## INFORMALITY AND IRREGULARITY

If nature is organic and an organic composition presents the opposite of a formal, rational, predictable structure, then so too must informality and irregularity play a significant role in London's urban character. This is most vividly conveyed in London's street plan, which largely retains its undisciplined and haphazard medieval layout that to this day remains diametrically opposed to the rational geometry of the rectilinear street grid (Fig.14). London's

14    The quaint misalignment of Clements Lane and St Edmund, King and Martyr Church (1292 [foundation]; 1670 [restoration]) in the City reflects the informal irregularity found throughout London's urban landscape.

layout therefore is emblematic of a city that revels in a form of organised chaos, a city whose urban landscape largely rejects the monotony and uniformity of controlled growth and imposed urban plans and revels instead in the easy spontaneity of an informal and irregular spirit. We see London's built fabric reflect this tradition time and time again. Varied street frontages, asymmetrical squares, kinked thoroughfares, diverse materials, stylistic variety and even more recently, London's chaotic skyline – all these characteristics conspire with London's innate propensity for diversity and contrast to forge a cityscape where, in built environment terms, almost anything is possible.

Of course, there are indeed moments of formality and regularity in the capital. Bloomsbury, Marylebone and Canary Wharf offer largely rectilinear street grids; Kingsway, Aldwych and the Mall present impressive formal urban set-pieces; and the spectacular Old Royal Naval College complex at Greenwich marks the triumphant realisation of baroque axial planning as forensic and precise as anything to be found in Vienna or Rome. But these instances tend to be the exceptions rather than the rules and by the time the imperial pomp of Aldwych has dissipated inevitably into the labyrinthine warren of narrow alleyways and crooked streets of Covent Garden next door, London's usual informal service has been resumed.

## HUMANITY

So, if we take these various characteristics now identified as being part of London's character and put them together, what are we left with? We have observed that London is diverse, volatile and mercurial. Its unplanned development also indicates a level of wilful unpredictability. It has intricate ownership hierarchies and democratic instincts that prioritise individual liberties over authoritarian control. It is an innately domesticated animal that cherishes intimacy and human scale. London also takes intense pride in naturalism and forces the man-made to bend to the will of the organic. And by so doing, London

15 An allegorical statue representing architecture cradles a miniature St Paul's Cathedral on Vauxhall Bridge.

displays intense regard for irregularity, promoting a chaotic sense of urban order.

How can we further summarise these characteristics? London is changeable, unpredictable, sporadically disorganised, complex, proud, individualistic, domesticated, intimate, natural and flawed. These descriptions inevitably point to one unavoidable conclusion: above all else, London is human. What do we mean by human? Every city in the world houses humans, so what makes London different? What is human about a city that has a population almost twice the size of Norway's, covers an area nearly 10 times the size of Monaco, has depressing levels of social inequality and latterly, regrettably, rising rates of crime? If London is human, then what does this say about humanity?

In architectural terms there is much to recommend London's humanity: the generally human scale of its buildings and spaces, the intimacy of its residential fabric, its individualistic approach to design and formality, the huge priority it gives to nature, its ability to disperse intimacy and diversity on a vast scale, its distillation of mass urbanisation into smaller, more accessible, village-sized chunks, its effective distillation of the 'mass' to the 'me'. All of these things speak of a city that, despite its colossal size, has somehow managed to promote a softer, more civilised, more human brand of mass urbanism (Fig.15).

But, as with people, it is not just in London's multiple successes, but in its imperfections that also we find the fragile fingerprint of humanity. We humans are not in ourselves predictable creatures, we are not formal, we are not planned, we are not precise: in short, we are not Paris. Humanity exists in corners and crevices, nooks and crannies; it is always richer and more genuine when cultivated and nurtured rather than calculated and contrived. Humanity is earned not summoned, perfect urban masterpieces do not and should not exist, by their flaws you shall know them. Like all the great men and women in history, London is a flawed masterpiece. But London's flaws are the same flaws we see in each and every one of us and this enables city and citizen to relate and respond to each other in a more intimate, more human way. It is this simple human exchange that is at the very core of London's character.

# London Falling: The Collapse of London's Character

The previous chapter attempted to define London's unique urban character. Today, much of that character is under threat from a variety of sources, which are summarised below (Fig.16).

## TALL BUILDINGS

While London's skyline is never likely to be completely transformed into the dense forest of high-rise towers that we see in Manhattan or Shanghai, it is undeniable that over the past two decades, tall buildings have irrevocably altered and very often, gravely undermined London's urban character. For the approximately 1900 years of its existence before the Second World War, London was a primarily low-rise city, so much so that at the start of the 18th century, an enchanted Peter the Great of Russia set about building a city inspired by the steeples and spires he had seen clustered onto the London skyline on his famous 1697 visit to England. That city is today known as St Petersburg and it now offers a more authentic representation of London's historic skyline than London itself.

Of course, during this 1900-year period London had individual high-rise landmarks; like all big cities London has always coveted buildings of scale for reasons of power and prestige. Over the past three centuries those landmarks have included the Palace of Westminster's 98 m (321 ft) high Victoria Tower and, most notably, the 111 m (364 ft) dome of St Paul's Cathedral, London's tallest building from 1710 until the early 1960s. In fact, with its colossal 156 m (512 ft) spire, Old St Paul's had been one of the largest structures in Europe and was the tallest building in the world up until 1311. So London is by no means a stranger to height.

16 The incongruous presence of 20 Fenchurch Street (2014) looming over historic Lovat Lane in the City provides a stark visual reminder of how London's historic character is being undermined by insensitive and inappropriate new developments.

17    Now barely visible beneath the wall of high-rises behind it, the swamping of the Tower of London reflects the wider harm several tall buildings have inflicted on London's historic character.

Equally, it is also true that the tall buildings that now threaten London have only been structurally and culturally plausible in this country since the mid-20th century. So it is disingenuous to a degree to solely present almost two millennia of low-rise development as automatic justification for an indigenous low-rise urban character when for the vast majority of that period the prohibition of skyscrapers was not a cultural choice but an engineering inevitability. But there can be now little doubt that London's traditional low- to mid-rise character is under threat. As of March 2019, a record-breaking 541 buildings of 20 storeys or more were proposed across the city, a six per cent increase on the previous year.[7] To encapsulate the surge, in the 33 years between 1968 and 2001, ten buildings taller than 150 m (492 ft) were completed in London. In 2019 alone, the number was 25.[8]

What impact has this explosion of tall buildings in a relatively short space of time had on London's character? In the main, it has been devastating. Key heritage assets such as St Paul's Cathedral and the Tower of London have been undermined and almost comically diminished by their immediate proximity to much taller structures. Historic Royal Palaces has already referred to the status of the Tower of London as that of a 'toy castle' due to the proximity of skyscrapers (Fig.17).[9] Important views across the capital have been thoughtlessly compromised, sometimes violating the prominence of national monuments. 22 Bishopsgate and the Leadenhall Building now crash into the famous view of the dome of St Paul's from Fleet Street; St George Wharf Tower joins the 1963 Millbank Tower in enjoying unwarranted prominence in views of Parliament and Westminster; and 20 Fenchurch Street (the Walkie Talkie) protrudes obscenely above the City from practically everywhere.

As a result, the integrity of London's historic fabric has been gravely compromised, particularly in the City of London, its oldest district. The indiscriminate and uncoordinated dispersal of tall buildings across the city has added a chaotic and disordered quality to London's urban form and blurred the individuality of its distinctive neighbourhoods. The poor design quality of many of these towers has also harmed the architectural impact and coherence of the city, chipping away at its global reputation as an iconic architectural centre.

Socially and environmentally, these towers have been problematic too. A staggering 90 per cent of the 541 tall buildings currently proposed for London are residential, a trend that has been commonplace for much of this century. With the majority of these towers earmarked for luxury accommodation or global capital investment (i.e. unoccupied), they have become totemic symbols of economic inequality in London and they embody the city's abject failure to reverse its current housing crisis. Even worse, they challenge London's long-fought tradition of social equanimity and stand in stark contrast to London's proud and pioneering early 20th-century social housing heritage.

Environmentally, tall buildings are generally less sustainable than smaller ones, with higher levels of energy consumption and energy inefficiency and sometimes prompting severe wind tunnel effects at their base, a development which caused particular alarm to City planners at 20 Fenchurch Street in 2015. Even New York City, the spiritual home of the skyscraper, is turning against tall glass buildings, with mayor Bill de Blasio recently hinting strongly that all glass skyscrapers in his city should be banned. But, worst of all, London's clumsy assimilation of skyscrapers has undermined its humanistic identity and has helped erode the special character, scale and intimacy that once made London unique.

Much damage has already been done, but what can be done to prevent further harm in the future? The answer is simple: London needs a definitive, coherent, city-wide, tall building policy framework that identifies where tall buildings should and should not be built, ensures they are of the very highest standard of architectural design and forensically analyses the impact of proposed tall buildings on skyline and townscape. It is incredible that currently no London-wide tall buildings policy exists, a shocking statutory oversight which is not replicated in virtually any other major city in the world. Moreover, cities with even more established high-rise centres, such as Frankfurt and New York, have long had similar frameworks in place.

Such a policy need not be a conservationist ruse to suppress tall buildings. For far too long, the husbandry of the London skyline has been naively caricatured by some as an ideological fight between conservation and development. All that such a policy would do would be to guide the development of tall buildings by maximising their positive, exhilarating impact and preventing them from inflicting harm. Without such a policy, London's skyline will lurch from one opportunist high-rise disaster to another, weakening the city's character at every turn.

## CONSERVATION

London is an old city and its historic fabric is an integral part of its character. This is not a prejudicial ploy to minimise the huge value and significance of contemporary architecture: it is simply a statement of fact. All historic cities need protections in place to ensure that new development can proceed without undue harm to heritage assets (Fig.18). But because London largely rejects the 'Old City' arrangement popular in Europe, where old and new buildings are quite literally kept apart, the onus on the capital to ensure the protection and endurance of its historic character is even greater.

Yet, alas, all too often, London's historic character is marginalised and undermined by architectural insensitivity or lack of statutory effectiveness. The indiscriminate spread of tall

18 Hasilwood House, by Mewes and Davis (1926), is one of the few remaining historic structures on Bishopsgate in the City and is virtually swamped by a sea of glass and steel.

buildings as discussed earlier is one example of the latter and London has frequently rejected UNESCO calls for the implementation of buffer zones around the Westminster and Tower of London World Heritage Sites that would limit the height of tall buildings within them (Fig.19).

But it is not just tall buildings that pose a threat to London's historic character: current statutory protection arrangements also contribute to the problem. There are currently two principal ways in which a neighbourhood or individual building can enjoy additional protection in recognition of their historic value: the listings process and conservation area designation. There are three grades of listing that can be awarded to a historic building: Grade I is in recognition of the highest value, followed by Grade II* and Grade II levels. The problem from a character point of view is that the setting of a heritage asset is not actively taken into account when considering whether that asset is suitable for listing, it is the architectural content of the building in question that is prioritised over all other considerations.

This policy has led to the demolition of a number of buildings that had made a significant contribution to the historic character of their surroundings, but were not considered architecturally significant or authentic enough to

19 The absurd overshadowing of Hopton's Almshouses (1749) by Neo Bankside (2014) in Southwark shows the complete lack of sensitivity and protection now frequently applied to London's heritage assets.

merit listed building status. In Hanover Square in 2017, Celanese House, a handsome, 1920s Portland stone classical building, was demolished to make way for 22 Hanover Square, a crude, prefab-like structure with form, massing and facades completely out of step with the historic grain and rhythm of the local area. While Celanese House may not have been architecturally significant in and of itself, it made a quiet and reassuring contribution to the townscape background of the square which has now been needlessly eradicated by a building of lower architectural quality and contextual sensitivity.

Cases like this occur all over London and each one marks a needless blow to the city's historic character. In theory, conservation areas are intended to pick up the slack and provide looser protections for historic or important neighbourhoods. But whereas the listing process can be too prescriptive, conservation area designation is often loosely defined and there are multiple examples of grossly inappropriate architecture built within them. Perhaps a new tier of protection is required to identify more assertively the contribution listed or unlisted buildings make to local historic character and provide the required level of protection therein. Renewing the built environment is only a sign of progress if the new building marks an improvement on what it replaces and does not inflict harm on the historic character of its setting. London is not a *tabula rasa*, it is not virgin territory, it is rich, dense, complex and old, and new architecture works best if it responds to this rather than ignores it.

20 With scores of luxury flats, no social housing and 52 storeys placed incongruously beside the key, low-rise, public asset of the River Thames, SimpsonHaugh's One Blackfriars (2018) is both a product and a symptom of London's housing crisis.

## HOUSING CRISIS

London is in the grip of a housing crisis. While the solution is complex and as yet unclear, the problem is very simple. London, essentially, does not have enough properties to house its growing population. As supply is low and demand is high, prices have risen. Prices have also risen exponentially because London property, particularly high-end London property, has been identified as a pre-eminently valuable and secure global asset, which has prompted an influx of foreign property investment into the city. Not only has this raised prices even higher, thereby worsening the initial demand and supply problem, it has triggered rampant residential redevelopment across the city. However, all too often, the residential developments being built are serving the high-end market rather than meeting the needs of ordinary, less commercially lucrative Londoners (Fig.20). Coupled with the collapse in the supply of social and affordable housing (albeit now being falteringly addressed),

London is left in a Faustian property pact: empty luxury homes and an insufficient supply of affordable housing.

This has affected London's character in two ways. The first is perhaps the most obvious and relates to the social consequences of the lack of affordable housing. Since the late 19th century, London has been a pioneer in the provision of housing for the very poorest in society, its Guinness Trust and Peabody Housing Estates are still in use today and spearheading the modern council estate, of which the Boundary Estate formed the first of its kind in the world. The inter-and post-war periods saw this legacy extended and, while mistakes were clearly made in 1960s and 1970s tower block housing, the heroic social egalitarianism that underpinned large-scale public housing ventures like the Becontree Estate merely extended London's reputation as a socially and economically mixed egalitarian hub. All of this is now under threat as new generations of Londoners are potentially priced out of their city. Gentrification remains a contentious term and it clearly comes with advantages and disadvantages. But the sheer pace at which it has already taken hold across London shows that the potential social and economic displacement of one set of Londoners in favour of another is a clear and present threat. The best architects in the world can do nothing for a city if its soul has withered, and London's soul is its people. If London is to have anything approaching the humanist reputation it enjoyed in the 20th century in the 21st, then it needs to ensure that the very rich can live side by side in the city with the less affluent, as has been the case for centuries.

The second way in which London's housing crisis has affected the city's character has been the explosion of non-affordable housing that burgeoning property prices have triggered. The pressure this has placed on the development of tall buildings has been discussed. But there are a number of other ways in which this has potentially affected the city's character. The first is overdevelopment. Such are the astronomical returns to be accrued from London development at present, that all development restraint is frequently abandoned in favour of irresponsibly testing just how much planners are prepared to let opportunistic developers get away with.

Enabled by an organically minded planning system that favours reactive empiricism over definitive constraints (as we have again found with London's lack of a tall buildings policy), schemes across London are being delivered where maximisation of floorplate is clearly the overriding priority above every other conceivable consideration. The most obvious examples of this trend relate once again to tall buildings, but there are various examples right across the city. Southbank Place, Bishopsgate Goodsyard, Lewisham Gateway, the redevelopments of New Scotland Yard and Broadgate – all these schemes threaten to unleash considerable harm on local and wider character and scale by stacking as many bland, steroid-enhanced blocks onto a site as possible to realise the investment returns required to justify the colossal sums spent on acquiring the land in the first place.

Another way in which London's housing crisis potentially impacts the city's character negatively is related to a process known as regeneration ransom. A developer commits to regenerating an area. So far so good. But the price, or 'ransom', for that regeneration (although of course it is never presented as such) might be the aforesaid overdevelopment, the demolition of a heritage asset, or the introduction of contextually inappropriate or insensitive architecture. Regardless of which type of ransom is imposed, it is always pitched as being a necessary evil for the delivery of the greater good of regeneration. Again, examples abound. We can perhaps trace the inception of the process back to the 1950s when the Hilton Hotel Group literally threatened to quit London altogether and thereby rob it of vital post-war economic regeneration unless their new flagship hotel at Hyde Park Corner – a clumsy protrusion of tepid Manhattan pastiche – was awarded planning permission. More recent regeneration schemes at Nova Victoria, Nine Elms and Woolwich Central have followed the same path. Urban regeneration should unquestionably be a positive thing. But when aligned to cynical ultimatums that have the potential to destabilise character, one begins to understand the suspicion and reluctance with which some residents and communities engage with those who would seemingly wish to improve their lot.

## DESIGN

Design is, of course, subjective. When *Private Eye* magazine awarded Will Alsop's Palestra Building in Southwark the Worst London Building Award in 2006, it promptly won a Royal Institute of British Architects London Award the following year. Equally, while 20 Fenchurch Street won *Building Design* magazine's Carbuncle Cup in 2015 for the worst building in the UK, it also won in the best commercial high-rise category in the International Property Awards of the same year. And yet, design is central to urban character. So, despite its inherent subjectivity, there must be established methods for quantifying whether it has a positive or negative impact. In London of late, partially prompted by burgeoning private housebuilding triggered by the housing crisis, much of its impact has been negative.

Travelling though London today, one can see any number of identikit design solutions (particularly on residential developments) that either actively or unwittingly suppress the rich diversity and quirky individualism that was once a key part of the city's character. One sees the same unitised cladding solutions repeated over and over again, the same sub-London vernacular brick panelling, the same crudely recessed upper storeys to suggest a building is shorter than it actually is, the same extraneous canopies to dumbly denote an entrance, the same bloated floorplates, the same squat, rectilinear blocks, the same sterile glass skyscrapers. For a city whose character has historically defined itself by the abject rejection of uniformity and monotony in favour of individuality and variety, it is depressing indeed to see so much London architecture lie prostrate before the authoritarian altar of anodyne anonymity (Fig.21).

What is the solution? There are many ingenious architects working in London today capable of producing wondrous work. But it is undeniable that there are others lacking the skills or application to convincingly respond to the richness of London's character in inventive and

21  Woolwich Central by Sheppard Robson (2014) won *Building Design*'s Carbuncle Cup prize for worst UK building (2014) and exemplifies the poor quality of much of contemporary London housing.

inspiring ways. There are inevitable pressures on architectural design, ranging from budget to client ambition to procurement route, but good architecture is about responding to context and constraints and not reacting against them. London needs to do better if it wishes to embrace the former once again.

Of course, it is not architects who are to blame for poor design, but planners who consistently let bad architecture slip through the net. In the halcyon days of the London County Council, London government had hundreds of planners in its employ: it is incredible to think that Leslie Martin designed the Royal Festival Hall while working for the LCC. London's latest concert hall, the Barbican Centre for Music, is being designed by the American practice Diller Scofidio + Renfro and it is all but unthinkable today that such a project would be essentially designed by a local authority. It is also interesting to note the priority that London's LCC successor, the Greater London Authority, gives to design. Transport for London, the city's public transport authority, employs almost 30,000 people. Design for London, a tactical unit established by the GLA to promote good urbanism, was disbanded in 2013 and at its peak employed just 25 staff. The comparison may be trite but it is telling – a city that does not invest in design cannot benefit from it.

Other than the roles played by architects and planners, there are also wider cultural impediments to the delivery of good design in London. Lack of affordable housing is frequently presented as a reason for denying housing projects planning permission and has been cited on scores of initially rejected high-rise proposals ranging from St George Wharf Tower to Newcombe House in Notting Hill Gate. This is of course a reasonable position to take, particularly in the light of London's housing crisis and also when considering that both schemes in question were woeful enough to be rejected by any means. But affordable housing is easily quantifiable and measurable: what about those other elements of design that are not? Who then is defending and promoting beauty in London's architecture? Who is defending and promoting the joy, elegance and inspiration that good design can bring? Who is dismissing proposals on the grounds that they lack

these ingredients? Yet beauty, like design, is in the eye of the beholder. And innate British pragmatism could perhaps never embrace the intellectual pursuit of beauty with the same tenacity and conviction as other more philosophically and romantically inclined European audiences. But unless London and the professional communities that serve it discover a mechanism that is brave and incisive enough to try and construct an idea of what an aesthetic vision for the city might be, then London's character will cease to benefit from a 'visual dividend' that its design communities neither covet nor understand.

## PUBLIC SPACE

Public space is the glue that holds London's character together. It is London's streets and squares that provide the physical canvas on which all the drama and energy of public life takes place. Over the past two decades, London has made great strides in embellishing its character with new and improved public spaces. The heroic redevelopment of Trafalgar Square in 2003 still arguably stands as the civic highlight, but in the intervening period scores of new spaces have joined London public space community. King's Cross has provided King's Cross Square and Granary Square, Leicester Square has been revamped, the UK's largest shared surface scheme has been laid out on Exhibition Road and the City's Street Scene Challenge has done wonders in terms of creating or revitalising under-utilised pockets of public space in the Square Mile. Further afield, Transport for London's ambitious infrastructure reconfiguration projects of previously inhospitable gyratories like Archway and Elephant and Castle have helped decongest key junctions across the city.

But still, all too often, public space and pedestrian priority in London is sacrificed to the needs of the car, a negation that does much harm to the reputation for humanity, inclusivity and civility that London's character historically maintains. Parliament Square remains one of the worst examples; it is laughable that the civic hub of the cradle of democracy is encircled by a gyratory of traffic and rendered virtually inaccessible due to the lack of pedestrian

22    Despite being home to the 'Mother of Parliaments', parts of Parliament Square still require pedestrians to take their lives into their own hands when trying to reach its central space.

crossings (Fig.22). Much the same situation exists at countless other locations such as Marble Arch, Hyde Park Corner, Euston Road, Park Lane and London Wall. The design of several of these locations stems from a generation prior to the more recent scope of this book. Nonetheless, if London is ever going to embark on any committed programme to define, protect and enhance its character, then healing its public space will have to be front and centre of such an undertaking.

# A Tale of Five Cities:
# Comparative Urban Set-Pieces

## LONDON VS BERLIN

### Altes Museum, Berlin

✦ **Architect:** Karl Friedrich Schinkel
✦ **Construction:** 1823–30

The Greek Revival form of neoclassicism found favour across Europe in the early 19th century and proved particularly popular in Germany where, in 1823, the same year as work began on the contemporaneous British Museum in London, K.F. von Schinkel commenced work on the smaller Altes (Old) Museum in Berlin. Straddling one end of Unter den Linden, the city's main boulevard, the museum is fronted by a large, formal square additionally enclosed by the Spree River, Berlin Cathedral and the reconstruction of the demolished Hohenzollern Palace – all of which combined to create a striking and very formal civic composition. The Altes Museum also forms the southern tip of Museumsinsel (Museum Island), the UNESCO World Heritage Site which includes an extraordinary ensemble of five other world-class neoclassical museum buildings (Fig.23).

23    The Altes Museum defines its surroundings.

24   The British Museum, by contrast, is constrained by its surroundings.

## British Museum, London

✦ **Architect:** Sir Robert Smirke, Sydney Smirke

✦ **Construction:** 1823–57

Despite the enormous similarities in architectural style and composition, the urban setting of the British Museum could not possibly be any more different from that of the Altes Museum and it says a great deal about the restrictions and opportunities London's character imposes on its architectural set-pieces. Unlike the Altes Museum and despite its colossal scale and monumental colonnades, the British Museum is squeezed onto a narrow Bloomsbury backstreet which seemingly belies the institution's size and status and forces oblique views of an architectural elevation conspicuously designed to enjoy the opposite. This incongruous

juxtaposition has also stubbornly survived repeated attempts to remove it. John Nash first proposed a grand, diagonal boulevard that would have linked the museum to Trafalgar Square and the GLC (Greater London Council) frequently toyed with the idea of flattening the warren of Georgian streets and terraces opposite the museum and erecting a huge public square that would have rendered it visible from the nearby main thoroughfare of Bloomsbury Way (Fig.24).

The survival of the museum's environs in their original state, as well as the continued frustration of plans to remodel them on a grander scale, are both indicative of wider traits in London's urban character. Although partially dictated by the historic location of old Montagu House where the museum's collections were initially housed, the modest setting for so prominent a public building

35

suggests a casual ambivalence towards the spatial and architectural rituals of formal civic display in the city. In their place, it also implies a preference for irregularity and informality as well as an inadvertent preoccupation with the use of contrast and friction as dramatic urban devices. The sudden, spontaneous, and occasionally surreal shifts in scale and massing this produces, forms one of the principal visual pleasures of walking around the capital. In London the unexpected can quite literally be around the corner. But perhaps the true lesson of the British Museum is that London is a city whose character instinctively responds to the grain and motion of its indigenous, irregular street pattern with an enthusiasm it does not necessarily extend towards the single architectural gesture, regardless of the scale and ambition with which that gesture is conceived.

The 18th-century architect Sir William Chambers understood this perfectly when designing Somerset House in the 1770s and 1780s. Despite its palatial scale and the operatic spatial mechanics of its sunken Piranesian courtyard spaces, he deftly concealed all this emotional volatility behind a noble yet deceptively unassuming street frontage facing the Strand. The compliant manner in which Somerset House thus engages with its streetscape therefore conforms more obediently to the rules of London's character than the more defiant British Museum which tries, and ultimately fails, to rebel against them. But even the failure of a hulking Greek temple humbled by the backstreets of Bloomsbury brings with it a drama and tension that further enriches and electrifies London's character.

## LONDON VS NEW YORK

### Lincoln Center, New York

- ✦ **Architects:** Philip Johnson, Wallace K. Harrison, Max Abramovitz, Eero Saarinen
- ✦ **Construction:** 1959–66

New York's Lincoln Center is one of the premier performing arts venues in the world. This remarkable modernist cultural complex houses some of the city's most eminent performing arts institutions and performance venues within a series of grand, whitewashed pavilions linked by a number of interlocking, travertine-decked, public plazas. Its glitzy centrepiece is the Metropolitan Opera House, a 3800-seater auditorium set behind a lofty arcaded foyer that glimmers at night like a jewel box. The 6.5-hectare (16.3-acre) Upper West Side complex has itself come in for a fair share of criticism, with renowned American urbanist Jane Jacobs once decrying the economic and political contrivances that promoted cultural 'segregation' of this kind. But what is undeniable, is

25   The Lincoln Center opens out towards its context.

the democratised openness and permeability of its masterplan, which seeks to wholly and inexorably integrate the complex into the surrounding city fabric and public realm. This enlightened approach is implemented with consummate architectural sophistication and is evident everywhere, from the broad expanses of foyer glazing that offer long views to and from the city, to the extraordinary civic generosity of its principal, fountain-encrusted Josie Robertson Plaza that serves as the gateway to the complex and in so doing, thrusts itself eagerly out towards Broadway (Fig.25).

## Barbican Centre, London

✦ **Architects:** Chamberlin, Powell & Bon
✦ **Construction:** 1965–82

The Barbican Centre is culturally and architecturally comparable with the Lincoln Center, with both being products of 1960s civic and artistic post-war aspiration and experimentation. Socially, however, the Barbican is far more ambitious and sets a significantly more egalitarian tone by not only placing its equally distinguished roster of eminent arts institutions on 24 hectares (60 acres) of bomb-devastated City land, but by surrounding them with housing for some 6500 people, initially allocated to City workers for rent. The fact that today its social housing function has been completely reversed into primarily luxury and exclusive residential accommodation does not detract from the genuine egalitarian spirt with which it was originally conceived. While its brutalist architecture does not necessarily chime with the tradition of humanist domesticity on which London's character is largely based, its founding social ambitions certainly did. But it is in the Barbican's urban composition and public realm where it diverges not only from the Lincoln Center, but also from many of the themes of openness and intimacy found in London's traditional character.

Whereas the Lincoln Center avidly embraces the city around it, the Barbican inexplicably severs itself from it, revelling instead in a futile social introversion that largely confines its cultural amenities deep into its sunken and famously

26   The Barbican Centre is surrounded by an oppressive and defensive perimeter.

impenetrable core rather than along a perimeter which could, potentially, have been animated by their presence (Fig.26). The subsequent treatment of this perimeter, with its forbidding, high-level fortress-like walls sparingly punctuated with 'gated' entrances, is also highly indicative of a development that resonates with the complex's nihilistic urban approach that effectively turns its back on the city. Detached from the life and fabric of the city in this manner, the barely 'public' spaces within the Barbican propagate the kind of sterile anonymity and anaesthetised detachment that is largely atypical to London's character and, for many Londoners even today, still renders the Barbican something of an unknown quantity.

Although the Barbican's negative features are largely anomalous to London as a whole, they do reflect wider trends that still represent a threat to London's character today. Isolationist design, urban impermeability, poor legibility and a maligned public realm are all elements that feature in some of the worst cases of inappropriate development in the capital today. The irony is that in the Barbican they coexist with much for which we should be thankful. Its (original) social and cultural progressiveness has already been noted, as has the sheer pioneering ambition of its post-war regeneration aims. Add to this the exemplary internal standard of its residential units, which all feature floor-to-ceiling timber doors and windows and highly efficient, spacious layouts. Additionally, though initially deeply unpopular, its uncompromising brutalist style has won favour and redemption amongst many for its sculptural purity and forthright form. Ironically, it is in this series of puzzling contradictions that the Barbican, complete with all its flaws and triumphs, represents something of the inconsistency of human nature which London's character as a whole, so fervently embodies.

## LONDON VS PARIS

### The Palais Garnier, Paris

+ **Architect:** Jean-Louis Charles Garnier
+ **Construction:** 1861–75

The sumptuous Palais Garnier opera house in Paris is perhaps the civic and architectural embodiment of the Second Empire Beaux-Arts ideal as zealously pursued by Napoléon III and his expedient Préfet de la Seine, Georges-Eugène Haussmann. Formally and symmetrically bejewelled in a vibrant, bustling square with wide, straight, tree-lined avenues radiating from it in all directions, the Palais Garnier is the star player in a lavish urban theatre production every bit as precise, scripted and melodramatic as those which take place within its gilded auditorium (Fig.27).

Even more so than Haussmann's totemic boulevards, the opera house represents the city as a work of monumental urban sculpture: it is a scheduled civic climax within an entirely planned, controlled and obedient urban framework whose every detail and permutation has been deliberately determined by conscious decisions and not left to organic empiricism – in effect nature's complete subjugation to man played out on an urban scale. It represents a typically Gallic conceptual pursuit

27  The Palais Garnier is the glittering centrepiece of a grand urban set-piece.

of urban order first initiated by the great baroque landscaper André le Nôtre 200 years earlier at – ironically – the gardens at Versailles. And it is a pursuit that, unsurprisingly, has largely proved complete anathema to London.

## Royal Opera House, London

✦ **Architect:** Edward Middleton Barry, Dixon Jones
✦ **Construction:** 1857–8, 1990–99

Work on both the Royal Opera House and the Palais Garnier was started within four years of each other in 1857 and 1861 respectively, but that is where the similarities end. While the Paris opera house is an urban juggernaut that sears its way into the physical fabric and civic consciousness of the city, the Royal Opera House assumes a deferentially avuncular presence on a quiet London side street and, beyond its immediate Covent Garden environs, enjoys virtually no physical impact on London's wider layout or fabric as a whole. In fact, so humble are its urban aspirations that rather than exploit its fortuitous proximity to the great Covent Garden Piazza right next to it to construct a dramatic civic set-piece, it turns its back on London's first formal classical public square and looks soberly onto a narrow, winding and largely insignificant thoroughfare instead (Fig.28).

The contrast between these two opposing methods of reconciling a prestigious national cultural venue such as an opera house with its surrounding urban fabric, says much about the differing urban characters of both cities. London's handling is indicative yet again of the city's generally more modest, informal and irregular approach to civic ostentation and also reflects its habitual reluctance to manipulate its organic street layout for the purposes of a single architectural set-piece or urban climax.

And yet, despite appearances to the contrary, the submissiveness of the Royal Opera House not only reflects London's character, but it helps influence it too. On the surface, the relative ignominy of its setting was sealed when, shortly after the opera house opened, a hall conceived to house an exotic fruit, flower and vegetable market (by the same

28   The Royal Opera House, conversely, opts for dignified solemnity on a side street.

architect no less!) was constructed right next door. Though devised to help raise funds for the opera house, the contrast between bourgeois elitism and proletariat toil could not be more pronounced. And yet it is also indicative of the porous and comparatively non-hierarchical social structure that London's urban fabric lends to its urban character, features that have helped nourish the perceptions of humanism often attributed to the city.

In having its own prominence denied, the Royal Opera House attempts instead to define its persona by means of progressive layers of subtle physical engagement with its urban context – weaving itself through the existing fabric of its surroundings over gradual increments of time. This is a process updated by the splendid 1990s restoration and extension as well as its more recent 'Open Up' refurbishment programme by Stanton Williams Architects, both of which finally provided new and expanded entrances directly from the piazza. Additionally, these schemes finally recruited the adjacent renamed Floral Hall as a spectacular glass recital hall for the opera house itself, an ingenious adaptation that has helped strengthen the institution's civic impact. This theme of subtle engagement is also present in WilkinsonEyre's sensuous, twisting, high-level 'concertina' bridge link to the Royal School of Ballet next door.

Within the confines of a built environment as structurally intransigent as that found in London, this kind of reciprocal architectural dialogue with surrounding context is frequently the most effective means by which new buildings can forge a clear civic identity within the otherwise unwieldy urban fabric. London essentially forces these buildings to grow into the city, asserting their validity by reference to what surrounds them rather than objectifying their own presence and persona. London's character essentially forces buildings to collaborate in order to make an impression, yet another human trait to which the city tacitly subscribes.

## LONDON VS ROME

### St Peter's Basilica, Vatican City

✦ **Architects:** Donato Bramante, Michelangelo di Lodovico Buonarroti, Gian Lorenzo Bernini and others

✦ **Construction:** 1506–1626

From its conception in 1506, St Peter's Basilica was planned as nothing less than the absolute physical apotheosis of divine glory as relayed through the combined earthly artifices of art and architecture. Its design was also eventually recruited as a stupendous propaganda vehicle for the new baroque style, an in-house artistic movement essentially invented by the Catholic Church to solidify the faith and combat the growing threat posed by the Reformation by giving sublime physical expression to the spiritual mysteries of the Catholic liturgy (Fig.29).

29    St Peter's Basilica monumentally imposes itself onto its surroundings.

As such, St Peter's was conceived on a Herculean scale and today is still the largest church in Christendom. As the centrepiece of Vatican City it continues to enjoy pre-eminent physical, psychological and political status across Rome, a position spectacularly reaffirmed by the addition of Bernini's stupendous colonnade and piazza of 1655–7 and Mussolini's controversial, though effective, Via della Conciliazione of 1936–50, the great 500 m (1640 ft) long avenue that sliced through the maze of historic structures in Rome's Borgo district in order to formally enthrone the basilica as the climactic epicentre of a colossal urban set-piece. Despite the tacit attempt to usurp its civic supremacy with the post-unification erection of the vast Victor Emmanuel II Monument between 1885 and 1936, St Peter's still dominates Rome's urban landscape and skyline to this day.

## St Paul's Cathedral, London

+ **Architect:** Sir Christopher Wren
+ **Construction:** 1675–1710

To no small extent, St Paul's Cathedral was partially conceived as a somewhat more rational Protestant reaction to the awe-inspiring emotional vehemence of its great liturgical rival, Catholic St Peter's in Rome. But St Paul's politically discreet but architecturally superlative adoption of the baroque style, inconveniently aligned to Catholicism, shows how closely, in fact, the two buildings are linked in both spiritual and design terms. St Paul's too was initially planned to dominate London's urban landscape, a role it continued to amply fulfil until the latter half of the 20th century. But whereas St Peter's dominance of the skyline remains, St Paul's has been thoughtlessly compromised by the unwarranted incursion of high-rise towers into its immediate vicinity and the wider cityscape that surrounds it.

This dilution of the prominence St Paul's once enjoyed on the London skyline does indeed say something about the loose and frequently irresponsible approach that is all too often taken to the protection of London's character. But more intriguingly, the unique manner in which the great cathedral is integrated into London's townscape and streetscape is richly reflective of the habitual traits and themes that define the city's character.

30   St Paul's Cathedral, by contrast, creeps tentatively into view.

As one approaches St Paul's from Fleet Street, its slow, almost reluctant, emergence into full view remains a compelling, intricately staged and subtly baroque urban sequence of concealment and revelation, typified by the captivating manner in which the slender lead steeple of St Martin-within-Ludgate church dances expectantly around the cathedral dome. This fluid, processional sequence is a far cry from the didactic, monumental clarity and precision we see applied to the approach to St Peter's. But it does firmly rest within London's more intimate urban design traditions of contrast, informality, sequence and surprise (Fig.30).

Much the same can be said of the buildings that line the Ludgate Hill approach. In their residential character, indiscriminate plot widths, textured diversity of colour, height and materials and relative lack of the stylistic uniformity one might expect in the vicinity of a nation's principal church, they clearly betray the fact that London possesses one of the least homogenous urban streetscapes of any European capital. However, behind this apparent disunity lurks the potential for two possible outcomes. The first is the proliferation of poor or insensitive architecture buoyed by a lack of prescriptive control and ultimately capable of eroding character and cohesion. But the second is the exact opposite and is signified by the variety, individuality, animation and interest that form the unforgettable backdrop to so many streets, squares and spaces in the capital and for which the city has become justly famous.

Within this hectic and layered spatial experience lies the lesson of St Paul's and Ludgate Hill. The urban form of London may initially appear too fragmentary and sporadic to force an immediate impact. But it does invariably achieve harmony through diversity and subsequently demands from its observers a more engaged and intuitive process of unravelling before it lays its riches open to view. Whereas other cities may assert their urbanity by compelling the observer to stand back and gape in awe, London casually dares its citizens to immerse themselves in the set-piece rather than admire it. Curiosity is rarely so rewarded.

# Part II
# Protecting London's Urban Character

The following components are the (primarily) physical ingredients used to construct urban character. Identifying them is the first step to protecting these core components and then harnessing them in any new development intervention.

- ✦ Alleyways
- ✦ Art
- ✦ Climate
- ✦ Colour
- ✦ Density
- ✦ Entrances
- ✦ Fountains
- ✦ Furniture
- ✦ Grain
- ✦ Grid
- ✦ Height
- ✦ Housing
- ✦ Lighting
- ✦ Materials
- ✦ Names
- ✦ Paving
- ✦ Planning
- ✦ Signage
- ✦ Squares
- ✦ Streets
- ✦ Style
- ✦ Topography
- ✦ Transport
- ✦ Uses
- ✦ Views
- ✦ Waterways

## ALLEYWAYS

Behind almost every grand street or frontage in central London lurks a sheltered labyrinth of routes and passageways that form the city's extraordinary network of alleyways. London is a city of contrasts, formal and imposing at one moment, furtive and clandestine the next. The latter condition is most forcibly expressed in the hidden ecosystem of alleyways that snake through the city. Alleyways are also joined by a fascinating backstreet hinterland of yards, courts, lanes, railway arches and passageways that form the prowling spatial understudies to the capital's headline urban acts.

These alluring ancillary spaces are critically important in understanding the layered intricacy of London's urban character for a number of reasons. First, alleyways are invariably, though not exclusively, historic and thereby provide a tantalising glimpse of old London. With their (modernised) gas lamps and bowed casement windows, alleys like Goodwin's Court in Covent Garden and Mason's Avenue in the City of London

32  The City of London is full of historic, atmospheric alleyways like St Michael's Alley.

offer a beguiling and picturesque conduit into the vanished worlds of Georgian and medieval London respectively (Fig.32).

Second, by their nature, alleyways are small and intimate; astonishingly what claims to be London's narrowest alleyway, Brydges Court in Covent Garden, is just 38 cm wide. For a city of London's colossal scale, to offer spaces of almost claustrophobic intimacy is a tactile and benignly oppressive physical concentration of the domesticated humanism that lies at the heart of London's urban character. Like London itself, alleyways are about the individual and not the whole.

33    Medieval Lovat Lane in the City dramatically frames a narrow view of the Shard.

The irregular layout of historic alleys in particular also reflects the wider organic composition of London's messy and undisciplined street grid. With their hidden corners, gentle slopes and constant twists and turns, alleyways, like Lovat Lane and French Ordinary Court in the City, revel in the surprise, spontaneity and genteel disorder that captivates London's urban fabric at large. They also show the variety inherent in London's urban environment and display a diverse mix of materials, roof heights, entrances and architectural styles (Fig.33).

And finally, in a sprawling modern megalopolis, alleyways are a reminder of London's rural origins and domesticated, village-like neighbourhood structure. For instance, the cobbled courtyards and narrow lanes of Mayfair's Lancashire Court and Shepherd Market mark so pronounced a spatial shift in scale and aspect from the aristocratic regalia of the surrounding neighbourhood that they almost appear airlifted in from a sleepy rural hamlet.

It is important for architects not to dismiss alleyways as antiquated relics of a bygone age but to appreciate their intrinsic value as dynamic urban conduits that can help integrate new developments into their surrounding physical and spatial fabric. It is a lesson that new developments like Victoria's Eccleston Yards, Covent Garden's Floral Court and the City's Chichester Rents have learned to both their and London's credit. For in their staggered routes, intimacy of scale, variety of form and spontaneity of streetscape, they strike deep into London's urban character. If you understand London's alleyways you understand London.

## ART

Public art forms a major civic component in the urban character of several major cities and the same is true of London. In one sense, London is not like Rome or Salzburg; it does not generally use art to convey emotional turbulence or political prestige in the tradition of many European cities. While hauntingly naturalistic statues on Gian Lorenzo Bernini's extraordinary Fountain of the Four Rivers in Rome's Piazza Navona literally shield their faces in awe of the papal power and baroque brilliance channelled by the sumptuous Sant'Agnese in Agone church beside them, London must contend with the rather more passive spectacle of Sir Edwin Landseer's iconic lions staring out with stoic impassivity over Trafalgar Square. But stoicism and passivity are elements of the national character which public art in London, historically at least, tends to reflect.

However, public art has still had a big impact on the city's urban character and public spaces. Eros (or more accurately his vengeful brother Anteros) has now kept his amorous watch over Piccadilly Circus for almost 130 years and, as well as being a superlative example of Victorian sculpture, it is one of the most famous landmarks in the city. The luxuriant gold leaf, applied to the monuments of Queen Victoria and her husband Prince Albert on their stupendous respective memorials in front of Buckingham Palace and the Royal Albert Hall, makes a dashing and decadent splash against the grey London skies and theatrically indicates the enormous role art has played in the ritual of royal commemoration played out in London's streets and public spaces for centuries. For over half a century Barbara Hepworth's *Winged Figure* sculpture on the side of the flagship John Lewis department store on Oxford Street has become a familiar landmark to hundreds of millions of shoppers from across the world and provides a pertinent reminder of the historic links between art and commerce. Equally, a host of monuments from

**34** *Angel's Wings* by Thomas Heatherwick (2002) provides a dynamic, contemporary counterfoil to Bishop's Court off Paternoster Square in the City.

Edward Baily's Nelson's Column to Christopher Wren's Monument in the City show the extent to which public art has been traditionally used as a military or historic commentator in the capital (Fig.34). The tradition continues today, even in abstracted form; the convoluted whorls of Anish Kapoor's Orbit structure in the Queen Elizabeth Park not only mark the London 2012 Olympic Games but have transformed the east London skyline and now constitute the tallest public sculpture in Europe.

But in this most ancient of cities, art now tends to be used not only to convey tradition or commemorate events but to reflect the blistering innovation and inventiveness that drives contemporary London's creative culture and is an intrinsic part of the city's character. Two of the most successful examples of this are the temporary commissions for the Fourth Plinth in Trafalgar Square and the Serpentine Pavilion in Hyde Park. By commissioning a rolling series of dynamic sculptural works within these hyper-historic settings, both programmes show London's openness to contemporary culture and the extent to which the capital covets contrast. Even more organically, in the wealth of changing street art on display in historic but heavily gentrified areas of Shoreditch and Spitalfields, art is used to expose the surprisingly strong vein of counterculture and nonconformity that runs through a city which is widely perceived as embodying the exact opposite.

## CLIMATE

Famously, London has a damp and rainy climate but this too has helped form its character. The greys and off-whites of the Portland stone buildings which adorn central London in particular, mimic the grey skies which frequently hover over the capital. This grinds the city's architecture into its context with the same visual fluency as the sun-kissed renders of Miami's multicoloured art deco pavilions reflect the sheen and glimmer of a city bathed in year-long sunshine. The greyness that often afflicts London's weather is a colour that speaks of dullness, seriousness and sobriety. While the first condition is one that cannot reasonably be

35    Rare moments of hot weather lead to London's parks and squares, like Lincoln's Inn Fields (1632), being colonised by a grateful public.

applied to the capital, the latter two, in stereotype if not necessarily reality, certainly can.

London's climate of tepid summers and relatively cold winters was one of the reasons given for the city's previous reluctance to fully embrace cafe culture. In recent decades, however, this has changed significantly, and many areas of London now foster a vibrant pavement cafe culture that endures in spite of the weather, with patio heaters now a common feature outside bars and pubs in the winter. If Copenhagen can accommodate such a culture, a city where winter temperatures regularly plummet to below zero (a relatively rare occurrence in London), then why not London too?

It is important, however, not to view London's rainy climate as having a universally bad impact on the city's character and culture. Fine, hot weather may pass unnoticed in cities with warmer climes

but, due to its rarity in London, it is seized upon with relish by the populace whenever it occurs. The impact is almost immediate as parks and public spaces across the city become colonised by hordes of relaxing Londoners desperate to enjoy every inch of their public realm on the few days of balmy respite the weather allows (Fig.35). On days like this the city literally becomes infected with so palpable a buzz of revelry and recreation that any prior civic propensity for sobriety vanishes entirely. Time will tell if such cosmopolitan enthusiasm can be maintained if global warming makes such weather events more commonplace in the capital. But, for the present at least, it is clear that the lack of sun energises London's character as much as the presence of it.

Something else London's changing climate has energised is the debate over air quality in the city. A 2014 King's College report claimed that on some days, Oxford Street was the most 'polluted street in the world'.[10] While significantly the report only measured one noxious emission (nitrogen dioxide), it starkly illustrates the extent to which air pollution is now an urgent environmental issue in the capital. Measures to reduce pollution promise to have a direct impact on London's character. The congestion charge was implemented in March 2003 to reduce traffic levels and air pollution and the new Ultra Low Emissions Zone (ULEZ), introduced in April 2019, essentially widens the net (and, by 2021, the area) to whom these charges apply. Less traffic in central London could open the door to a radical reappraisal of the way public space is used in the city. We have already seen this with the installation of an ambitious, if controversial, cycle lane network across central London and, if lower car use facilitates further pedestrianisation, then the environment could be responsible for radically rejuvenating London's public realm.

Air quality is perhaps the most prominent civic demonstration of the inexorable rise of the sustainability agenda in recent years. Last year, London itself played host to a series of mass climate change demonstrations and it is generally now accepted through all strands of society that cities must be at the forefront of the drive to create a healthier and more sustainable future. While London is part of the C40 group of cities that has pledged to reduce carbon emissions by 60 per cent by 2025, other cities have gone even further. The mayor of Paris has pledged to pedestrianise huge swathes of the city if re-elected in 2020 and Copenhagen is committed to reducing carbon emissions to zero by 2025. But what of the impact of sustainability on London's character? Overall, this can be considered in positive terms and we have already seen how environmental measures in London can improve both air quality and the public realm. But there is a potentially negative impact. The term 'embodied carbon' refers to the amount of carbon dioxide emitted during the construction of a building, so the bigger the building, the greater its embodied carbon. It is now generally accepted that, in order to retain embodied carbon, redundant buildings should generally be refurbished rather than demolished. While this makes perfect sense

in sustainability terms, it does not necessarily make sense within a townscape context and many buildings that make a negative contribution to local townscape and character that might otherwise have been removed when leasehold tenancies expired, are now finding their lease of life injudiciously preserved in order to mitigate against the potential emission of embodied carbon. Arguably, the most significant example of this in recent years has been Howard Fairbairn and Partners' monstrous Portland House in Victoria which, despite its 29 storeys being utterly at odds with the surrounding historic streetscape and incongruously undermining the setting of key iconic heritage assets such as Buckingham Palace, has gained approval for redevelopment and extension under 2018 plans partially approved on the grounds of the unacceptable release of embodied carbon were the building to be demolished. Scores of other similar examples exist. Of course, adaptation and reuse of existing buildings must take priority, particularly in a city where historic buildings make such a significant contribution to the city's character. But if sustainability is to be used as a Trojan Horse to secure the unwarranted retention of buildings that harm urban character, then it may well offer the dire, unintended consequence of preserving bad architecture and planning mistakes in perpetuity.

## COLOUR

Alfred Hitchcock once bemoaned that, in London, 'the sky was always grey, the rain was grey, the mud was grey and I was grey'.[11] The great director may well have been taking cinematic licence to disparage a city he actually loved but he was tapping into popular perceptions of a monochrome northern European city afflicted with sullen hues and a damp and rainy climate.

Portland stone takes great responsibility for Hitchcock's disdain and has historically been the definitive material for the vast majority of London's grander buildings. While it obviously lends monumentality and permanence to London's character, it can vary from an off-white pallor to a more limestone grey, usually depending on age. Hence many London buildings are indeed grey, and it forms one of the defining architectural colours of the capital, so much so that when Renzo Piano was designing his first London building at Central St Giles, completed in 2010, he decked it in an orgy of pulsating colours to form a joyful polychromatic riposte to what he perceived as London's more neutral tones (Fig.36).

But there are tones other than grey. London is primarily a city of brick, and the buff yellow of London stock brick is synonymous with all areas of London. Red brick too is widespread, particularly in central London. Grey even makes a reappearance on the blackish-stained Georgian terraces of Bloomsbury and Fitzrovia, where centuries of atmospheric discoloration have stained their original buff shade. Grey also makes a comeback on the glass and steel facades of some of the modern office buildings in the City and West End. An intrinsic part of London's character, however, is its subdivision into a number of distinctive neighbourhoods, and one of the most endearing parts of that character is the manner in which buildings in a particular neighbourhood assume a specific colour to help craft their own individual identity. For instance, Regent's Park, Belgravia and Bayswater are forever associated with the creamy yellow stucco of their distinctive Regency and Victorian terraces. And the Cadogan Estate in Chelsea and parts of Kensington is known for its vivid collection of blood-red brick or terracotta buildings. It is also London's neighbourhood configuration that does most to challenge the perception of London being a grey city. Historic villages like Primrose Hill and

36  The grey and white Portland stone of the Bank of England (1791) and 1 Princes Street (1929) in the City dominate much of central London's visual townscape.

37  The pretty coloured terraces of areas like Portobello Road (above) and Primrose Hill defy London's reputation for grey pallor and enliven the city's character.

Notting Hill on the periphery of central London frequently display terraces emblazoned with a riot of pinks, blues, yellows, reds, purples and greens (Fig.37). This once again reaffirms the picturesque domesticity at the heart of London's urban character, here transforming the urban backdrop of one of the biggest cities in the world into a warm, pastoral facsimile of idyllic village life.

It is also important to remember that the colours that define London's urban character are not solely to be found on its buildings. If any one colour was to form an emblem of the city it is arguably the red in which its buses, fire engines, postboxes, tube train roundels, telephone boxes, Yeoman Warders or 'Beefeaters', Queen's Guards and Chelsea Pensioners are decked. At the opposite end of the decadence scale, the black livery of London taxis and police officers' uniforms reiterates the sense of sobriety and endurance with which London's urban character is so often associated. And, of course, London's wealth of parks and affinity with natural landscapes make it a green city, and trees form the consistent, softening backdrop to the city's urban fabric. So London is actually a more colourful city than you, or Hitchcock, might think.

## DENSITY

Density is essentially the measurement of how many people live, on average, in any square acre, hectare, kilometre or mile in a city. On one level it is a superfluous statistical strapline that has about as much influence on the everyday life of the common man or woman as radio waves or the price of gold. But considered more broadly, density is the critical demographic regulator that determines how people are dispersed across a city and consequently how that city looks and, more importantly, how it feels. Population statistics tell you how many people live in a city, but density begins to give you an idea of how they live. It is therefore critical to urban character and, to a lesser degree, urban form as well.

Despite its size, or perhaps because of it, London is a famously low-density city. For every person within one square mile in London, there are almost two for the same area in New York, three in Barcelona, four in Paris and a staggering twelve in Manila. This brings with it advantages and disadvantages. The key advantage is an asset that strikes at the heart of London's character: for all its size, London feels like an innately human and liveable city. Its low density provides the city with a spaciousness and breathability that is a key part of its humanistic urban appeal and enables neighbourhoods in a vast city to still successfully subscribe to village-like intimacies. The lowest densities may well be concentrated in the rows of terraced houses that are more a feature of suburbia than they are of central London. But the entire city benefits from the culture of civility and individuality they help enforce.

In cities like Los Angeles which are unduly reliant on the motor car and have only a vaguely defined centre, one of the biggest disadvantages of low density is its promotion of urban sprawl. While this does not apply to London, one disadvantage that does, is low density's propensity to foster inefficient use of space which then hikes up pressure and prices on available land for development. Inevitably, this then increases the likelihood of inappropriate development, an affliction from which London is currently suffering greatly. But low density is also an issue of character as well as land use. Cities are about the activity, buzz and compression that high densities engender. We may instinctively process crowds and traffic as irritants, but deep down they

remind and reassure us that we are within the urban condition or, more subconsciously, that we are not alone. If low densities unduly dilute these stimulants, then we lose something of the thrill of living in a city.

So the ideal urban condition is one which can effectively manage both low and high densities, where areas of tranquillity and activity can exist side by side. Ironically, in the past, London has been largely successful in achieving this, but current pressures threaten this delicate equilibrium. As a result of the city's current housing crisis there is a strategic drive to densify the city. One of the most corrosive consequences of this has been the proliferation of tall buildings alleged to provide the 'super-densities' required to provide the housing that London needs. But studies have consistently shown that it is actually the mid-rise typology that creates the greatest densities. Paris and Barcelona use the apartment block typology to achieve significantly higher densities than London with virtually no residential tall buildings, and the densest borough in London, Kensington and Chelsea, maintains a conspicuously low-rise townscape.

Kensington and similar areas like Victoria and Marylebone often achieve their high densities through typologies like the mansion house block, an Anglicised version of the European apartment block. These are normally handsome, Victorian and Edwardian red-brick blocks of flats that rise to around seven or eight storeys but whose efficient layouts and long ranges are able to achieve astonishingly high density ratios. They form an endearing and intrinsic part of many areas of London and they perhaps hold the key to contemporary London achieving high densities through architecture that enhances rather than endangers urban character. Happily there are an increasing number of examples of this kind of development in the capital and contemporary schemes like DSDHA's Abell and Cleland in Westminster and Sheppard Robson's Camden Courtyards skilfully reinterpret traditional London housing motifs such as courtyards, communality and balconies to establish a contemporary form of high-density living that is sympathetic to the city's heritage and character (Fig.38).

38   New developments like Camden Courtyards in Kentish Town (2017), follow London's historic mansion block tradition by optimising density within a mid-rise building template.

Table 1   Population Density of some UK and Global Cities

| Inhabitants per square mile | |
| --- | --- |
| Manila | 184,570 |
| Mumbai | 73,837 |
| Paris | 55,673 |
| Barcelona | 40,000 |
| New York | 27,000 |
| Tokyo | 16,120 |
| London | 15,400 |
| Portsmouth | 13,365 |
| Manchester | 11,439 |
| Birmingham | 10,391 |
| Los Angeles | 7,544 |
| Cardiff | 6,400 |
| Glasgow | 3,521 |

## ENTRANCES

If eyes are the windows to the soul, then entrances are the eyes of architecture. Entrances make buildings human and legible; they are not just physical portals providing access to interiors, but they enable us to relate to our built environment more closely by shrinking architecture down to a human scale and managing the critical interaction between public realm and private space. Therefore, in a city that places as much human emphasis on intimacy and accessibility as London, they become hugely important (Fig.39).

With its rich and varied architecture, London offers infinite types of entrances. The City of London reveals theatrical, neo-baroque entrances dripping with statuary and ornamentation; the ambassadorial townhouses of Belgravia, Bayswater and South Kensington provide endless enfilades of stately stucco porches; the Victorian terraces of Hackney and Haringey feature

39 Expressive and decorative historic entrances, like this one on Drapers Hall (1772) in the City, provide a vital opportunity to humanise architecture and create character.

40 Another example of an ornate entrance, this one at 7 Lothbury (1866) in the City.

paired recessed porches flanked by rendered bay windows; and the office blocks of Canary Wharf sport shining glass entrance canopies constructed from a web of skeletal steel. Away from buildings, London also offers a wealth of more unconventional entrance types ranging from the decorative metal cages that once provided access to underground toilets to the ornamental arches and volutes that enclose the entrances to grand West End arcades (Fig.40).

Consequently, the type, style or design of entrance deployed is not necessarily important;

what is important is that the entrance be defined at all. Buildings without clearly defined entrances inadvertently sever themselves from the public realm and isolate architecture from its users, ultimately undermining the character of the city. Complexes like the Barbican, the adjacent Museum of London, a succession of 1960s office blocks and even newer developments like much of what is being constructed at Battersea and Vauxhall, suffer from this negation, and each one marks a wasted opportunity to enrich the character of the city by making it seem just a little less faceless and anonymous.

## FOUNTAINS

While London's temperate climate means it can never match the scale and drama of fountains in the hotter cities of Spain, Italy and Greece, which were historically used for cooling as well as ornamental devices, the British capital still offers a host of historic and contemporary fountains that form a key part of its character. Each one adds a playful touch to the cityscape and provides an alternative natural counterfoil to London's built fabric, other than the more customary choice of trees and natural landscaping.

Undoubtedly the most famous are the iconic fountains in Trafalgar Square where, in a practical diminution of civic ostentation that is typical to London, Charles Barry's original fountains were also devised as convenient, crowd-clearing devices for the potentially unruly groups that would

gather in the vast square for protest. Today Edwin Lutyens's 1930s replacement fountains appear more ostensibly benign and form the playful backdrop to an infinite number of picture postcards and tourist memorabilia of the city. In another more recent and somewhat irksome diminution of civic ostentation, despite being renovated in 2009 to shoot jets of water up to 25 m (80 ft) in the air, environmental restrictions enforced by the Greater London Authority commonly keep the jets at around only a quarter of this height. One dreads to think what the GLA would think of the 140 m (460 ft) plume Geneva's Jet d'Eau produces (Fig.41).

Less famous historic fountains include those at the base of the Eros statue in Piccadilly Circus and the baroque pools and jets subtly integrated into the plinth of Buckingham Palace's stupendous Queen Victoria Memorial. London's Royal Parks also offer an array of historic fountains including

41  Edwin Lutyens's 1939 remodelling of Trafalgar Square's original 1841 fountains are arguably the most famous in the UK.

42    Pavement-level water-jet fountains, such as those at Granary Square in King's Cross (2012), have become increasingly popular in London since their inception at Dixon Jones's dramatic overhaul of Somerset House in 2000.

the Triton Fountain in Regent's Park and, even more impressively, the Italian Fountains at Hyde Park, a formal composition of four terraced pools, each one fitted with and surrounded by spouting jets and set against a backdrop of the spectacular, natural landscape.

Sadly, public fountains fell out of favour in London for much of the 20th century, although the 1992 Horses of Helios sculpture and fountain on the corner of the refurbished Criterion Theatre on Piccadilly Circus quickly became an irrepressibly popular public landmark. It says much of the unique distribution of responsibility between London's public and private realms in the late 20th century

that one of the most famous public fountains of the era came from the private, rather than public, sector.

A bigger and significantly more influential boost to London's fountain compendium came with the opening of Dixon Jones's converted Somerset House in 2000, the centrepiece of which was a grid of 55 jets of water set level with the ground and capable of shooting synchronised plumes up to 4.5 m (15 ft) in the air. These were London's largest new fountains since the opening of Trafalgar Square and not only do they remain immensely popular today, they kick-started an enthusiastic trend for paving-embedded fountains that still grips the city today and has arguably become its de facto fountain type.

Similar fountain systems have now been installed in Granary Square, More London, Queen Elizabeth Olympic Park, the Victoria and Albert Museum, the Royal Academy of Arts, Russell Square, Leicester Square and, as part of seasonal installations, the South Bank. With the manifest opportunities these types of fountains provide for play, immersion and interactivity, they provide a dynamic valve for London to express the capacity for humanised informality and individualistic expression that lies at the heart of its urban character (Fig.42).

## FURNITURE

Street furniture serves two purposes. The first and most obvious is practical: bollards provide safety and security, lamp posts emit light, railings define boundaries and regulate access, litter bins promote cleanliness, benches offer rest, etc. The second and more interesting purpose, is the role they play in unifying the public realm and expressing the character and identity of a place or a city.

Historically, London's best example of street furniture that convincingly executes both roles is the Embankment, and today it still sets the symbolic benchmark to which all other developments should aspire. The Victoria Embankment was built in the late 1860s and marks one of the greatest infrastructure projects of the Victorian age, reclaiming land from the edge of the Thames on which to build a sewer and an underground railway covered by a new riverside road and a generous series of new public gardens. As one might expect, it is marked by all manner of gregariously decorated Victorian street furniture ranging from benches to lamp posts (Fig.43). But what makes the Embankment special is that the decoration applied to virtually every single piece of street furniture is carefully designed to reflect the river beside which it stands. Dolphins are wrapped around the base of lamp posts, cast-iron benches have swans for arms, smiling cherubs ride on galleons and brandish tridents on the King George V Silver Jubilee Memorial and, in one of the Thames's most romantic civic gestures, lights are strung between lamp posts on the river's edge to evoke the impression of a twinkling seashore. So strong is the tradition of decorative symbolism on the

43   With its swan benches and dolphin lamp posts, the marine-inspired Victoria Embankment (1869) provides one of London's best examples of visually and thematically consistent street furniture.

Embankment that it incorporates subtle variations too; on the benches near Cleopatra's Needle, sphinxes replace swans on the arms of the benches.

The Embankment shows the extent to which street furniture can be used to theatrically construct an aesthetically coordinated public realm based on a strong visual narrative that reveals the heritage and identity of the location in question. By deploying street furniture to essentially symbolise place, urban character is inevitably enhanced. Moreover, the Embankment is not all about imagery, the sculptural quality of its street furniture and the positioning of its benches on stepped plinths in order to permit better views of the river, remind us that good design is as crucial to successful street furniture as visual consistency.

London offers a selection of contemporary examples of coordinated street furniture that aspire to the Embankment's quality. The stainless steel overhaul applied to Kensington High Street in the 2000s attracted widespread praise and the work of landscape architect James Corner (creator of New York's celebrated High Line linear park) at the southern half of the Queen Elizabeth Olympic Park introduced an exemplary level of visual coordination

44   The new Queen Elizabeth Olympic Park (2012) features a unified and dynamic compendium of contemporary street furniture.

45   Incredibly narrow building plot widths along Fleet Street in the City reveal the enduring intricacy of London's urban grain.

and cutting-edge creativity to the street furniture compendium installed there (Fig.44).

However, all too often in London, the huge potential of street furniture to enhance streetscape and express character is wasted and the public realm becomes submerged beneath a morass of clutter. This happens at some of the city's most prestigious locations, as the plethora of road signs and traffic lights that litter Parliament Square and Euston Road shambolically attest. As so often in London, the lessons are in the past and, when it comes to answering the question of what role street furniture can play in enhancing urban character, the superlative Embankment offers all the answers we need.

## GRAIN

Urban grain refers to the size and pattern of individual plots within an overall urban block. For instance, a street of terraced townhouses may feature long, monumental rows of tall buildings. But as each row or block is divided into several small individual segments in plan, such a block

would be considered to have a fine urban grain. London, historically at least, tends to maintain a very fine urban grain and it is a key component of the city's character (Fig.45). This grain is essentially a result of two things: one urban, the other legal. First, it exists because of the stubborn (but welcome) persistence of London's organic and irregular layout, still in many older areas a labyrinthine, medieval concoction. And second, it exists because of the historic strength of individual property rights in English law. If after the Great Fire of London King Charles II himself was unable to coerce the merchants of the City to abandon their individual plots in favour of the mega-blocks destined for Wren's classical reconstruction plan, then few others were likely to succeed (Fig.46).

The consequences of this fine grain generate some of the most stirring urban pleasures

St Michael's Alley in the City provides a fine example of London's urban grain.

47 The narrow, vertical and varied composition of frontages on streets like King Street in Covent Garden is typical of London's fine, tight, historic grain.

London has to offer. Whereas in Paris the vertical presence of individual plots is submerged beneath the uncompromising horizontal sweep of the Haussmann terrace, in London, each individual plot is allowed to enjoy a visual presence on the street scene, creating a succession of vertical facades that subtly mimics the disordered variety of a line of multicoloured garments hanging along a wardrobe rail. Variety is a key issue here and it is directly encouraged by the reliance on smaller-scale commercial development. Adjacent plots were often owned by different landlords who employed different architects to build them at different periods, leading to even minor streets revealing an extraordinary variety of colours, styles, materials, heights and roofscapes. Throgmorton Street in the City of London, South Molton Street in Mayfair and Carnaby Street in Soho provide some of the most picturesque examples of this practice (Fig.47).

Inevitably, this leads to an impression of London that is more intimate, irregular and informal, features that are deeply embedded into London's urban character. It also creates a more humanly scaled city, and one whose streets, like its housing, provide a communal concentration of individualism. It is regrettable, therefore, when this delicate grain is ignored in new developments. There are scores of examples, but the Bloomberg Building in the City and Nova Victoria are two of the worst offenders. The fault is not entirely theirs; both buildings replaced horrendous post-war podium and slab developments which, with the help of wartime bombing, had obliterated the ancient grain that once existed beneath them. Equally, the accretive nature of modern commercial development does not help as it may involve a landlord lying in wait for years while patiently acquiring individual plots until the entire block is purchased and wholesale demolition and redevelopment may proceed unhindered. But, by schemes like Bloomberg and Nova adopting a scale, footprint and proportions that speak much more to the buildings themselves rather than the grain and rhythm of the streets around them, an opportunity to further enhance the character of the city by stitching its buildings more securely into its fabric is wasted.

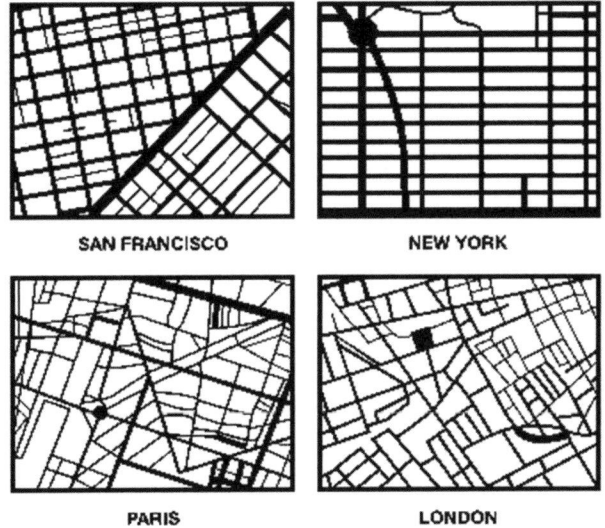

48   In comparison to other major cities, London is remarkable for largely retaining its sprawling, irregular medieval street pattern.

## GRID

London's layout proves that it is the absolute antithesis of the formal planned city. Whereas the maps of Barcelona, Manhattan and Paris reveal a precise, almost mathematical grid of orthogonal streets and rectilinear blocks either radiating from urban nodes or perpendicular to them, London for the most part presents a frenetic, uncontrolled sprawl of crooked, winding streets stumbling through a loose and irregular urban layout. If Manhattan's streets can be numbered, then by comparison London's are a veritable periodic table of coded, molecular urban confusion. In as much as London has a grid, it is one of the most undisciplined grids of any large city in the world (Fig.48).

There are a number of reasons for this. Certainly, London's oldest district, the City, largely retains its medieval street layout even though centuries of redevelopment have constantly changed the buildings that stand within it. Also, throughout London's long history it has tended to remain free from autocratic control, a remarkable feat for a European capital. In Second Empire Paris, Baron Haussmann and Napoleon III could literally make the city bend to their will, but in London Charles II could only watch helplessly on as City merchants ignored Wren's lavish post-Great Fire reconstruction plans and stubbornly rebuilt their premises on the same plot boundaries that existed beforehand. Consequently, as a result of London's relative political stability and independence, it has strenuously resisted any attempt to impose the kind of formal regimented plan favoured by its contemporary European and American cities. The one significant exception to this was John Nash and George IV's great Via Triumphalis, but even here, the sweeping Regent Street vista was forced to shuffle, twist and turn through London's chaotic streetscape on its path from Buckingham Palace to Regent's Park. Moreover, the great palace Nash planned to construct for the king as the route's northern terminus was never built (London Zoo stands there today) and Nash himself was forced to become part-speculator and buy up tracts of land along the route for the development.

There are occasional pockets of orthogonal order in London's layout. Central London's great northern swathe encompassing Marylebone,

COPPA

49    London's irregular, organic street grid ensures that even tiny side streets can offer big surprises.

Fitzrovia and Bloomsbury is about as close as London gets to a formal grid. But, tellingly, these were not the result of a monarch's absolutist town planning decree, but of private, commercial speculation by London's great aristocratic estates. Equally, the symmetrical formality of the Mall, Waterloo Place/Lower Regent Street and Aldwych/Kingsway also represent relatively rare moments of axial precision. But, in the main, London's layout remains gloriously organic, a teeming, gyrating mass of sustained geometric awkwardness.

Clearly, this has a profound impact on London's urban character. The ingrained tradition of informality and irregularity we see in so many elements of London life – its architecture, its public spaces, its planning system, its skyline – has its core origins in London's unruly layout. Equally, the ability of London neighbourhoods to convincingly subscribe to the 'village' typology so endearingly associated with parts of the city, is a direct result of its informal, irregular plan. It would be harder to conceive of Wimbledon or Hampstead as villages were they marked by wide, tree-lined boulevards and formal radiating avenues. In fact, from its layout at least, London at times appears to be one giant, inflated village with metropolitan ambitions rather than the other way around. Consequently, these informal, village-like aspirations immediately bestow upon London an intimacy and accessibility that belie its great size. Formality arouses awe but informality invites interaction and interaction lies at the core of humanity. London's informal layout ultimately therefore, renders it a more human and approachable city. In its crooked streets and awkward junctions we see the flaws and imperfections of our own human nature and are immediately drawn closer to them as a result.

This is why, of all cities, London most rewards the curious. When standing at one end of Broadway in New York and seeing the great thoroughfare scythe its way through Manhattan like a hot knife through butter, one immediately gets a fairly comprehensive sense of the totality of the city. You need not visualise what distant stretches of Broadway might look like because, even if obscured by infinite perspective, you can pretty much see them. London's layout ensures

that no such street or facility exists. With its endless nooks, crannies and bends, London is a city that must be grasped in fragments, it unravels itself slowly, like opening a parcel or peeling an onion rather than immediately exposing itself like a showgirl jumping out of a birthday cake (Fig.49).

Walking through London is therefore a highly intuitive and immersive experience full of spontaneity and surprise. With all the conventional civic nods and winks that tell you what is going to happen next conspicuously absent from the script, what we have instead is a guerrilla game of hide-and-seek, a grand, sequential urban theatre composed around alternating patterns of concealment and revelation. Turn a corner and you might see a post office or a palace, a cafe or a cathedral; London's crazy-paving layout quite literally ensures that anything goes. Which is why, despite its occasional allusions towards rustic gentility, London's irregular layout in fact helps generate an urban character that bristles with kinetic melodrama and spatial surprise.

## HEIGHT

For the time being, London remains a primarily low- to mid-rise city with occasional instances or clusters of high-rise buildings. The vast majority of suburban London is low rise and principally constitutes two-storey terraced, detached or semi-detached housing. This composition helps explain London's remarkably low density; while London has roughly the same population as New York City it covers an area twice as large. This preponderance of low-rise buildings is also a significant factor in the sustenance of London's intimate, residential character as it helps dismantle the capital's enormity into more digestible, human-scaled parts.

Mid-rise buildings can be considered those ranging from approximately four to twelve storeys and it is into this category which the overwhelming majority of buildings in central London fall. In suburban London, town centres, employment centres and business districts will primarily comprise a mixture of low-rise buildings with mid-rise being adopted for key civic, retail, leisure or commercial structures. Wood Green in north London provides a typical example. Its main high road is a mixture of two- and three-storey buildings but its northern end is overlooked by a ten-storey civic office block and a seven-storey block of flats located above a shopping centre. This townscape pattern can be found across London.

Though central London has significant low-rise expanses, in its Georgian terraces for instance, it is dominated by mid-rise buildings. A typical West End side street such as Bedford Street in Covent Garden, will feature buildings of around four or five storeys, and a typical, primary West End thoroughfare such as Regent Street or Piccadilly, will accommodate buildings of up to seven or eight storeys. Even in more residential parts of London's centre, mansion blocks will also often reach the same height; those dotted around the southern borders of Hyde Park can reach up to ten storeys high. This greater concentration of height in the centre of London adds the necessary cosmopolitan hulk and gravitas to the heart of the global city but does so in a manner that still exerts horizontal rather than vertical form and retains a human-scaled relationship with the street and pedestrian.

The definition of high-rise or tall buildings varies wildly and, while statutory convention in London of late has been to consider anything above 20 storeys high-rise, the more internationally regarded standard is anything over 12 storeys. This marks a significant shift in a building's relationship with the street, city and pedestrian. For the first time, the building is beginning to exert more of a vertical force than a horizontal one, effectively peeling away from the ground-level fabric of the city and deliberately exerting itself as an isolated object. For a city that prizes human intimacy and domestic scale, this has significant ramifications. From the mid-20th century onwards, tall buildings in London were primarily clustered in central London, particularly the financial district of the City of London. During this period, the vast majority of London remained primarily, if not exclusively, low and medium rise. This changed in the 1980s when a second cluster of tall buildings was introduced in the new financial district of Canary Wharf. Since Canary Wharf's creation, the trend has turned again and, today, tall buildings proliferate across the entire city.

While tall buildings can obviously bring exhilaration and excitement and powerfully reinforce the scale and dynamism of the urban condition, their integration into London's traditionally low- to mid-rise fabric has often had a disastrous impact on the city's urban character. The seeds of dissension were sown in the first wave of high-rise construction in the 1960s, where the insensitive design and location of several tall buildings wrecked the historic character and composition of swathes of central London. Some of the worst offenders remain New Zealand House, Portland House Victoria, the London Hilton Hotel, Hyde Park Barracks and Millbank Tower, all of which violently interrupt the intricate tapestry of low- and mid-rise classical streets and squares that surround them and cause irreparable harm to local historic character, continuity and streetscape. Sadly, it is a toxic mantle that has now been enthusiastically assumed by a new current generation of tall buildings, with skyscrapers, like 20 Fenchurch Street and St George Wharf Tower, proudly sporting an equally catastrophic relationship with their immediate and surrounding townscapes (Fig.50).

Part of the problem has also been that central London has now effectively exported its laissez-faire approach to high-rise development to the rest of the city. In fact, it is the outer London boroughs reporting the biggest surge in tall building proposals, of the 541 tall buildings currently proposed for London, a third are in the outside central and inner London.[12] Incredibly, London has no city-wide tall buildings policy, so tall buildings are no longer limited to their loosely defined clusters in the City and Canary Wharf, but they now appear indiscriminately across the capital. In fact, the cluster arrangement, which is widely accept as the most sensitive and visually coherent way to arrange tall buildings certainly within a historic context, is often abandoned in favour of a more haphazard and uncoordinated sprawl of individual high-rise buildings in painfully incongruous suburban locations. This is why historically low-rise neighbourhoods like Swiss Cottage, Ealing, Barnet and Chiswick are coming under increasing pressure from the threat of high-rise development, an advent which promises to wreck London's residential, village-like character. Astonishingly, the skyline of

suburban London features significantly more tall buildings than that of suburban Los Angeles, where strict zoning laws, as in most American cities, limit high-rise development to downtown (central) business districts alone.

Of course, it might be possible to accommodate tall buildings in London more successfully. London is a big city and like all big cities has always coveted buildings of scale for reasons of power and prestige. Until the construction of the Eiffel Tower, the 52 m (170 ft) Nelson's Column was the tallest monument in both London and Paris, and the colossal 156 m (510 ft) spire of Old St Paul's was one of Europe's tallest structures. In fact, up until 1311, Old St Paul's Cathedral was the tallest building in the world. Even the present St Paul's is built on a vast scale and for 250 years has dominated the City skyline like an aircraft carrier surrounded by rowing boats. But there is a crucial difference between skyscrapers and St Paul's: the former articulate multiple storeys across a vertical form and therefore contradict human scale while the latter, thanks to its giant classical order, is essentially articulated as a two-storey volume which can thereby maintain a relationship with human scale and remain horizontally anchored into the city. Until London develops a coherent, city-wide tall buildings policy framework that prioritises high-quality design and is able to successfully consolidate London's conflicting height vs heritage aspirations, tall buildings in London will continue to wield significantly more harm than good.

## HOUSING

If we acknowledge London as one of the most humanist of big cities, then its approach to how it houses its population is central to both this claim and the city's character. London houses millions of people but, unlike Paris or New York, the majority of them live in houses rather than flats. Almost 9 million people live in London and they live in just over 3.5 million residential dwellings.[13] Of these dwellings, 58 per cent are houses with the remainder being flats.[14] This compares to New York where, of its 3.4 million dwellings, less than 9.5 per cent are houses with the remainder – a vast majority of over 3 million – being flats.[15]

Of the 58 per cent of London dwellings that are houses, terraced housing forms by far the largest contingent, 47 per cent. Semi-detached and detached houses account for 39 per cent and 14 per cent respectively.[16] This housing mix has had a profound impact on London's character for two reasons. First, houses tend to project more individuality than flats, they represent the infinity of the urban condition reduced to a more scalable bite-sized chunk. This intimacy of domesticity combined with the emphasis on the individual rather than the collective (at least in residential terms), has an extraordinarily civilising effect on mass urbanism and is an absolutely core component of London's character and appeal.

Second, the statistics also make clear that the terraced house is the definitive London housing type. Many other cities have their own linear dwelling-house equivalents: New York has its brownstones and Copenhagen and Amsterdam their row houses. But it is London where the terraced house or townhouse has become the de facto residential emblem for the city. This has partially been achieved by its synchronicity with another iconic London urban template, the square (see 'Squares'). London's tradition of residential terraces configured as a physical backdrop to garden squares also indicates the extent to which nature is harnessed as a recurring contextual theme within London housing. This is a theme that comes to enthusiastic fruition (albeit in detached and semi-detached rather than terraced form), in the landscaped parks, streets and squares of Hampstead Garden Suburb, London's seminal contribution to the Garden City movement of the early 20th century.

The variety of the terrace typology also reflects the diversity, egalitarianism and versatility of London housing stock and, by extension, its urban character. A terrace can be an identical procession of sumptuous Mayfair townhouses piled five storeys high and part of a monumental architectural frontage expressly designed to resemble a palace elevation. It could be a modest Edwardian side street with bay windows and gable ends where everything from hanging baskets to brick colour is deployed to express individuality rather than conformity and tacitly encourage chance encounters between neighbours. It could be a row of irregular, multicoloured cottages on a cobbled mews charmingly reminiscent of a rustic village lane. Or it could be scores of other terrace subsets in between. Each type performs the same London housing trick, it uses the terrace to redefine the street as a linear courtyard which can accommodate any level of privacy or engagement that each resident demands within a flexible visual template that encourages individual expression within the communal whole (Fig.51).

Contemporary architecture has also provided imaginatively updated versions of the terraced house for the next generation of Londoners. At Pinnacle N10 in Muswell Hill, pH+ architects playfully reinterpreted the traditional Edwardian townhouse; at Vaudeville Court in Finsbury Park, Levitt Bernstein dynamically remodelled a traditional London terrace; and at Signal Townhouses in Greenwich, AHMM skilfully reinvented one of the most discredited forms of all housing, the back-to-back house (Fig.52).

Of course, there are other forms of housing within the city and these too have had a significant impact on its character. Almshouses are a much-loved historic form of housing where 'U'-shaped

51  Historic Georgian terraces like those on Gower Street still remain an incredibly popular and familiar housing model for the capital more than 300 years after they were first erected.

52  Signal Townhouses in Greenwich (2018) by AHMM architects forms an ambitious contemporary reinterpretation of back-to-back terraced housing, a historically discredited residential typology.

rows of cottages will normally be arranged around a sheltered landscaped courtyard open to one side. The cottages are usually occupied by the more vulnerable members of society as historically, almshouses were the result of private or public endowments designed to help children, the elderly, the poor or the sick. Once again, they stress London's fine tradition of social benevolence and, in their intimate scale and garden setting, they are another opportunity to underline the genteel domesticity and quiet naturalism that helps define London's urban character.

Though only 42 per cent of London housing is flats, rapidly increasing land values and a strategic drive for higher densities has meant that the number is growing exponentially. Between 2010 and 2015, of the new-build housing created in London, a staggering 89 per cent were flats.[17] The consequences of this are a denser, more cosmopolitan and more concentrated city with, if flats are provided as part of genuine mixed-use schemes, increased pockets of animation and activity.

In London, flats exist in multiple forms. Historically, the archetypal London flat type is the mansion block, typically late Victorian or Edwardian, with communal entrances to the street. Internal cores, usually built of brick, and often with balconies and bay windows, maintain the appearance of a large single and architecturally coherent public building. In terms of London's character, the last point in particular is the key to the mansion block's success; they are able to house a large number of people with external amenity space and impressive density ratios within an architectural template that embeds itself effortlessly into the scale, rhythm and proportions of London streetscapes. Contemporary architects are finally cottoning on to their intrinsic value and the mansion block typology is being creatively reimagined for the 21st century by new schemes like Sergison Bates's 79 Fitzjohn's Avenue in Hampstead and Maccreanor Lavington's South Gardens, part of the massive Elephant & Castle regeneration.

While we now typically associate council estates with their controversial 1960s and 1970s incarnations, in London they have a much earlier and more positive heritage and were contemporaneous with the development of the mansion block. Early 20th-century council estates essentially attempted to extrapolate and multiply the principles of the terraced house across a multi-storey template and were often extremely successful at doing so. With their sheltered courtyards encircled by private and deck-access balconies and entered through a sequence of formal arches, landmark estates like the Bourne Estate in Clerkenwell (itself recently upgraded) presented a highly civilised model of mass urban social housing founded on the same principles of individualised communality that define the terrace, but with a more pronounced emphasis on community and interaction.

Other flat typologies are perhaps less successful. Despite notable exceptions like the Barbican and Trellick towers, for many, the tower block is still appraised in negative terms, inextricably associated with the sprawling council estates of the 1960s and 1970s, Bourne's brutish successors. Many, though not all, of these estates promptly developed a host of architectural and social problems including insufficient maintenance, hostile design and high levels of antisocial behaviour. Consequently, they became synonymous with extreme urban deprivation, severely tarnishing London's reputation for humane domesticity. Today, many of these developments are in the process of being demolished and redeveloped but this too presents problems for London's character. In terms of design, much of London's new generation of flats is bland and repetitive, frequently expressed as a series of faceless anodyne blocks whose floorplate-driven ubiquity has now blurred the distinctiveness and individuality of London's neighbourhoods. Cynically, many wrap themselves in sheaths of brickwork in order to superficially subscribe to the New London Vernacular style (see 'Materials' and 'Style').

London's astronomical house prices have also triggered an explosion in high-rise development, unleashing punitive and unnecessary townscape upheaval across the city. Even worse, the vast majority of these towers are luxury, thereby encouraging social as well as physical severance by feeding the resentment of the majority who cannot afford them and patently failing to address London's housing crisis (see 'Height'). This is a narrative made all the more toxic by the Grenfell

Tower fire in 2017, a disaster which could yet arrest the resurgence of residential high-rise blocks in the city. Encouragingly, there are several fine examples of contemporary housing in the capital, with architects like Peter Barber and Matthew Lloyd trying, through projects like Worland Gardens and St Mary of Eton, to recapture and reinvent some of the traditional principles of enclosure, intimacy and materiality that once defined London housing and the wider character of the city.

A final key aspect of how London's housing affects the character of the city is the social porosity it brings. London is a city of rich and poor but one of its key characteristics is the closeness with which the two groups coexist. To a large extent, it is only the wealthy who live in the centre of Paris, with the poor ignominiously housed in the ghettoised *banlieues* that encircle the edge of the city. This introduces clear social divisions studiously ingrained along physical and geographical lines. But in London, pockets of social or council housing are located in even the wealthiest parts of the city and, conversely, the suburbs accommodate a wide range of residential values. Clearly London has its housing problems and the disparity between rich and poor is frequently a source of them, but this is not ingrained in the city's plan.

Currently, it is primarily historic council housing that accommodates central London's low-income residents. However, as this central social housing stock is barely being replenished, rising prices and falling local authority budgets will inevitably restrict new, low-income residents from moving into the centre and place intense redevelopment pressure on these already scarce affordable housing sites. Evidence of this constriction already exists: in the 2000s the UK enjoyed a boom in city centre residential populations, with the amount of people living in Liverpool, Birmingham and Leeds increasing by 181 per cent, 163 per cent and 150 per cent and respectively between 2002 and 2015. In central London, by comparison, the population only increased by 22 per cent over the same period.[18] Nevertheless, London's porous social mix says much about the inclusive and egalitarian character of a city willing to deploy its urban fabric as a social leveller. In London a prince may live next to a pauper. It is a humane domestic equanimity that the city loses at its peril.

## LIGHTING

If Paris is the City of Lights, then London is perhaps defined by a kind of grudging luminescent pall that owes far more to municipal necessity than civic display. Night-time lighting of streets and buildings is a simple and relatively inexpensive way of making an enormous contribution to the visual excitement of a city. Not only can it illuminate elements of a city's character such as fountains, roofscapes or bridges, but it can theatrically transform and re-present the urban landscape to invigorate and electrify the pedestrian experience of a city at night. Christmas illuminations are extreme and specific example of this process, but they are based on the same core principle of visual reinterpretation and transformative dramatisation that conventional lighting offers (Fig.53).

As a whole, London is a reluctant subscriber to these values. Vast swathes of the city whose streets and buildings would benefit enormously from coordinated night-time lighting slip into darkness after the sun has set. For instance, the broad imperial sweep of Whitehall and Horse Guards Parade, the Gothic cluster of Parliament Square, and even Big Ben and the Palace of Westminster themselves would all be classic candidates for a coordinated lighting strategy that could recast familiar landmarks in a new and dynamic light. Or it could at the very least render them visible at night. But alas, all too often in London, the opportunity

53  Subtle and sophisticated lighting schemes, such as this one at Granary Square, demonstrate the enormous capacity good lighting has to deliver dramatic night-time landscapes and enliven urban character.

54    King's Cross Square also demonstrates the effects of good night-time lighting.

is wasted. A convenient excuse for this negation has often been the environmental threat of light pollution. But new LED technologies render this less of an issue and in 2006 the floodlighting of the east front of Buckingham Palace was replaced with state-of-the art LED lighting, which not only led to a lighting solution that was energy efficient but also low maintenance, less intrusive using a tenth of the electricity of conventional bulbs.

In other instances where the opportunity for night-time illumination is grasped, the effects are instantaneous and dazzling. The Crown Estate's incremental regeneration of Regent Street has yielded multiple dividends but one of the most dramatic is the thoroughfare's night-time transformation into a stunning parade of glowing classical frontages, thereby rendering its monumental Edwardian architecture all the more

dramatic. Knightsbridge benefits from a similar approach as do St James's Park, Westminster Abbey, the South Bank and, neon gregariousness aside, Tower Bridge. But much more could be done, away from landmark monuments and in the main thrust of London squares and high streets, to use night-time lighting to forge a coherent visual narrative that dramatically exposes the core physical characteristics that make a space, street or building unique (Fig.54).

## MATERIALS

London is a city whose buildings offer a rich mix of materials but, first and foremost, it is a city of brick and stone. Brickwork dominates in residential and suburban London and features

55   While brickwork is arguably London's de facto historic building material, new architecture like O'Donnell + Tuomey's Saw Swee Hock LSE Student Centre (2014) reveals that it can also be put to dynamic contemporary use.

extensively in central London also. Geologically, brickwork is indigenous to the capital and was traditionally formed from soft London clay. Brickwork became popular in the wake of the new building regulations introduced after the Great Fire of London in 1666 when timber was effectively banned as an external building material in favour of the more fire-resistant brick and stone. Georgian London took the cue and built scores of London's iconic residential terraces from the material. But it was the rapid expansion and suburbanisation of London that took place in the 19th century that led to much of the modern brick townscape we see today, with high streets, public buildings and especially thousands of rows of terraced housing being constructed from brick, leaving an indelible imprint on the city's urban character.

Of all the bricks used in the capital, London stock is the definitive brickwork of the city. Yellow, chalky, rough-hewn and pockmarked, its soft tones, miniaturised scale and mottled, dimpled texture are themselves poignantly emblematic of the imperfect, domesticated humanism riven deep in the city's urban character. Brickwork has also enjoyed something of a resurgence in popularity in recent years, with a new generation of London housing in particular being constructed from the material. With their sculptural articulation, repetitive elevations, unadorned facades and strong rectilinear massing, new brick buildings like Portobello Square by PRP architects and Cambridge & Wells Court by Lifschutz Davidson Sandilands are sometimes referred to as the New London Vernacular (see also Fig.55).

Unlike brick, stone is not indigenous to London and has historically been transported into the city. Nonetheless, since the Great Fire of London it has been London's default material for buildings of consequence. Portland stone is the most common example and it is to London's landmark public buildings and principal thoroughfares what London stock brick is to the capital's housing. From St Paul's Cathedral to Somerset House, Regent Street to Whitehall, Bank Junction to Trafalgar Square, Portland stone dominates the centre of the city like no other building material (Fig.56).

Other stonework features less extensively. The warm, beige hue of Bath stone is to be found in pockets of the city, most notably on the John Nash frontages of Buckingham Palace. Clipsham stone, another similar yellow limestone variant of Bath, famously decks the Palace of Westminster. Lighter sandstone dressings also date from Saxon times and feature on buildings like the Tower of London and St Pancras Station and Hotel. The Victorian and Edwardian periods also saw a host of buildings which combined brickwork and stone, with the latter being used as a decorative dressing with which to adorn the former. Some of the most famous examples of these are Westminster Cathedral and, again, St Pancras.

While granite is a familiar material in northern British cities, it features less on London buildings and is often used as a dressing or accompaniment, or limited to ornamental architecture, as is the case on Nelson's Column and the Duke of York's

56   Historically, the Portland stone of Sir Aston Webb's Admiralty Arch (1912) remains London's default material for buildings of note.

Column. Only on rare occasions in London does it form the principal external material, most notably perhaps on Tower Bridge and in shimmering reflective form on the art deco facade of Soho's Palladium House. For all the popular connotations of London being a grey city, its preponderance of off-white limestone and yellow brickwork means the opposite is often the case. Therefore, extensive use of granite's brooding dark tones tends to form an incongruous and relatively rare addition to the city.

More exotic stonework often comes in the form of terracotta and marble, the latter stone being so rarely deployed in London's damp climate that the city's most famous ornamental arch has been named after it. Terracotta enjoys greater exposure, particularly on major Victorian buildings such as Harrods, the Victoria and Albert Museum, the Natural History Museum, the Royal Albert Hall and the old Prudential Assurance Building. Terracotta has also proved popular with modern architects, possibly due to its ability to be fired into a wide range of colours, as buildings like Renzo Piano's Central St Giles and GMW's 28 Chancery Lane prove.

Modernity has also introduced metal and glass into London as external building materials. As a collective, these types of buildings feature most extensively in the financial districts of Canary Wharf and the eastern ranges of the City of

London, where glass and steel is deployed on a number of skyscrapers and office buildings. In the Victorian era, glass and metal were synonymous with the Industrial Revolution and the age of the railway, and some of London's greatest vaulted spans, such as Leadenhall Market and the train sheds of St Pancras and Paddington stations, feature roof glazing set within riotous extravaganzas of cast or wrought iron.

Stucco and render also feature as a popular external material finish in several parts of London. Perhaps most famously, stucco is the defining material used for Nash's Regent's Park terraces, whose palatial yellow neoclassical facades combine with the park's rich green foreground to form one of London's most stirring urban vignettes. Stucco also features on the ambassadorial neoclassical terraces of Belgravia, Pimlico and South Kensington and is applied in a softer, more informal manner on the multicoloured terraces of Notting Hill, Primrose Hill and Chelsea.

Concrete has made a prodigious contribution to modern London and, in its precast form, can assume the honed, sculpted quality of stone. However, though the recent renewed appreciation for Brutalism has helped rehabilitate concrete's reputation, it can still be a divisive and controversial addition to London's urban townscape (particularly when applied at scale) and will, in the minds of many, be forever stigmatised as an intruder into the crumpled charm of old London.

## NAMES

Names matter. While street naming conventions differ from city to city, each convention chosen says something about the city in question. Americans usually like the streets numbered to reflect the geometric purity of their grids. Cities in the Latin world are fond of naming their streets after important military or political events or historical dates to reflect the strong tradition of symbolic commemoration that persists in their national psyches. Paris names its streets after individuals of note; everyone from American presidents to English kings and prime ministers is thus commemorated there, including of course, the customary hordes of French historical figures.

As with so many things, London takes a more unique and relaxed approach. As opposed to those cities which have a strong tradition of symbolic naming, London is far more likely to be literal in its naming conventions and it is much more common for a street to be named after the practices that took place there rather than the date or individual that helped generate it. Places like Shepherd Market, named after 18th-century developer Edward Shepherd, are a rare exception. Interestingly, the etymology of the neighbourhood where it stands is far more typical of London. Mayfair is thus named after the riotous annual May Fair that took place there in the 18th century, a debauched, proletariat spectacle of such legendary proportions that the horrified local gentry were only able to suppress it after literally building the aforesaid Shepherd Market buildings right on top of the open field where the fair was once held.

Even London's nickname says something about the city in both literal and symbolic terms. The 'Big Smoke' emerged as London's preferred metropolitan moniker in the 19th century, a reference to the crippling pollution with which the Industrial Revolution and Victorian expansionism had smothered the city. It also acted as a meteorological reference to the thick fogs that once hung like a pungent pall over London and which, with typical London linguistic alacrity, were referred to as 'pea soupers' due to their gloopy consistency. The Big Smoke also acted as a convenient metaphor for the Great Smog of 1952, a toxic, air pollution-driven yellow fog so severe that not only did it kill an estimated 4,000 Londoners, but rancid odours and gases wafting into the Palace of Westminster from the adjacent Thames conspired with the appalling death toll to compel Parliament to pass the landmark Clean Air Act of 1956. Symbolically, the nickname also helps reflect something of the character of a city that revels in the opaque, organic and amorphous rather than the clear, formal and ordered.

So what does London's literalistic naming convention say about the city's wider character generally? As with so many other aspects of the city, it suggests an ingrained informality and a reluctance to engage in more bombastic civic tropes, elements equally evident in a range of London features ranging from its urban layout

57 Absurdist literalism is a feature of many London street and place names.

commonly nicknamed as gherkins, cheese graters and walkie talkies and the appellation is not always intended as a compliment. Equally, it is not by accident that Hyde Park's *Route de Roi* (King's Road) was phonetically corrupted into today's Rotten Row.

This literalistic naming tradition also augments London's character by adding a rich linguistic cadence to the street scene that enhances the simple pleasure of walking around the city. There is almost a lyrical, percussive quality to street names like Lamb's Conduit Street and Balls Pond Road and these resonant, elocutionary inflections greatly heighten the sensory stimulation that London offers. The names given to new developments can therefore be an effective way to embed the scheme in the linguistic traditions of the city, which is why avenues in the City's new Bloomberg Building and Victoria's Nova, named eponymously and rather unimaginatively after billionaire magnate Bloomberg himself and a former council leader, represent something of a missed opportunity.

to its public spaces. It also infers the confusion and illogicality once again prevalent in London's undisciplined layout and organic development; the nonsensical surrealism of names like Crutched Friars and Man in Moon Passage have confounded and delighted Londoners and visitors alike for centuries (Figs 57 and 58).

London's quirky naming tradition is also something else that makes the city seem more accessible and human. Calling a grand boulevard after a person in the Parisian tradition may sound like a humanistic gesture, but if the person in question was a distant general or king then it may appear more of a barrier than a bond. Naming a street after the products sold there, such as Poultry, may be decidedly more prosaic, but it is instantly more relatable. And finally, the tradition also speaks of the latent irreverence and nonconformity that lurk in London's character and street culture. Today, tall buildings are

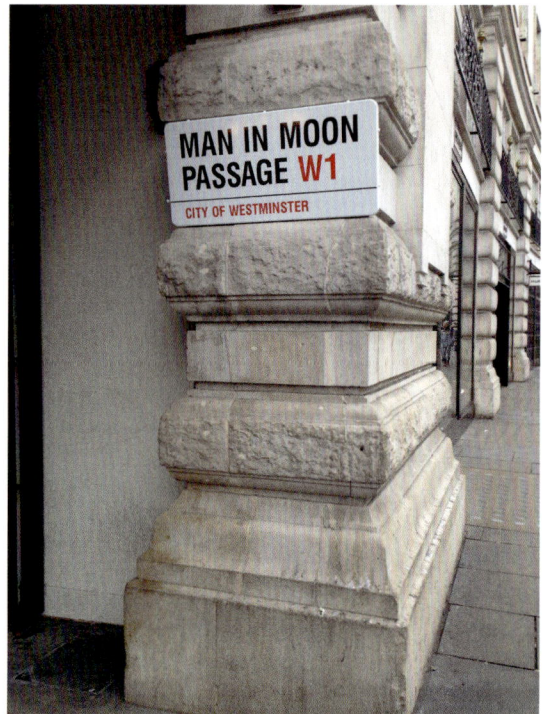

58 Each unusual name underlines the tradition of quirky irreverence sewn into the city's character

A brief explanation for a sample of London's most beguiling and baffling street and place names is offered below:

## Charing Cross

When Eleanor of Castile died in 1247, her grief-stricken husband King Edward I ordered the construction of twelve memorial crosses to her across the country. The French inscription *chère reine* (dear queen) was eventually corrupted to today's Anglicised 'Cha-ring'. The location for London's original cross was near to where the modern Charing Cross Station stands today on the spot occupied by Trafalgar Square's superb Charles I equestrian statue by Hubert Le Sueur. It remains the point from which all road distances to London from across the country are measured.

## French Ordinary Court

This atmospheric City alleyway marks the location of a popular medieval inn serving French Huguenots where a fixed-price meal was known as an 'ordinary'.

## Ha Ha Road

Woolwich in south-east London is not particularly renowned for its amusements and this narrow road is named after the old English word for a sunken boundary wall designed to permit unobstructed views – in this case of the adjacent Woolwich Common.

## Lamb's Conduit Street

Alas, nothing to do with lambs, but in true London fashion wonderfully weird and whimsical all the same. William Lambe paid for the construction of a new water conduit here in 1577 bringing fresh water into the City of London.

## Loampit Vale

'Loam' refers to the sandy clay soil found in the fields of north Lewisham in the 18th century and 'pit' recalls the limestone quarries once located there. The vale indicates this road's position at the foot of a gentle hill. The idyllic rural references contrast strongly with this traffic-filled, hard-edged south London artery.

## Shepherd's Bush

Allegedly, shepherds approaching London from the west once grazed their sheep on the fields here while driving their cattle towards Smithfield Market.

## Threadneedle Street

The 'Old Lady of Threadneedle Street', is the affectionate colloquial moniker for the Bank of England. The street name apparently derives from the haberdashery tools used by members of the Worshipful Company of Merchant Taylors whose livery hall is located off this narrow but famous City thoroughfare.

## PAVING

While London's streets are rarely paved with gold, what lies beneath our feet makes as much of a contribution to London's urban character as the walls and spaces around us. Accordingly, London has many different types of paving, all of which combine to help form an image of the city. Sadly, many of London's cobbled streets were ripped out in the mid-20th century and replaced by the infinitely less alluring, though indisputably more practical, tarmac. But there are still a handful of beguiling examples in areas like Soho, Mayfair, Covent Garden, Greenwich and the City of London and, like brickwork, cobblestones' intimate size and rough-edged, uneven surface always says something of the human-scaled domesticity of the city at large.

What is now much more common in London, is the ubiquitous concrete paving slab that forms the inevitable foreground to infinite visual impressions of the city. While visually these are unremarkable, their geometric setting-out and visible wear provides a reassuring sense of timelessness and

59  Dixon Jones's ambitious reworking of Exhibition Road (2011) has given the paving of the UK's largest shared-surface public space a jazzy, diagonal stitch.

firmness to the experience of walking through London. The pavement lights, often set into them to light basement spaces in central London in particular, inject a surreal, subterranean subtext to the pedestrian experience too.

There are, however, more interesting alternatives available. While granite makes a more limited impact on London's buildings (see 'Materials'), it is increasingly playing a bigger role in its paving, and granite setts are a popular contemporary choice for many new public spaces such as Granary Square, St James's Market and Archway Gyratory. Both neat and natural, they provide the perfect solution for developments wishing to evoke both modernity and tradition. Yorkstone paving provides a similar effect in a sandstone version and normally to a grander and more formal scale, as seen in Trafalgar Square and the Duke of York Square in Chelsea.

As this is London, there are always charming anomalies. Gravel makes an unexpected

appearance in Bedford and Fitzroy Squares, a crunchy reminder perhaps of the rural origins of their aristocratic landlords. Similarly, Horse Guards Parade never shies away from the fact that its first role is as parade ground rather than civic set-piece and it is covered, defiantly, in sand, another telling nod towards London's naturalistic affinities. Nearby, lies one of London's most enigmatic paving gestures, the red tarmac of the Mall. While its famous pigment was chosen to resemble a red carpet regally unfurled towards Buckingham Palace, it also shows that, despite popular perceptions to the contrary, London's urban character is well attuned towards ceremony, theatricality and performance when it chooses to be.

These are elements that also make an impact in one of London's most distinctive contemporary paving designs. Exhibition Road is the largest shared surface scheme in Britain and was transformed thus by architects Dixon Jones in 2011. With its bold diagonal criss-cross linking the various cultural institutions on either side of the street, it unfurls like a giant patchwork quilt from Hyde Park down to South Kensington. It is as jazzy and meticulously tailored a gesture as a Savile Row suit being worn inside out to reveal the decadent, multicoloured cross-stich inside and it shows that the civic counterpoint to London's perceived stiff upper lip is a cheeky and irreverent grin (Fig.59).

## PLANNING

London's planning hierarchy is complex and archaic, but it is key to understanding how London's character is either protected or threatened. Excluding the City of London there are 32 boroughs in the capital and each one can set its own autonomous policy for protecting its urban environment and promoting development within its boundary. This presents the first obvious problem, there are essentially 32 feudal mini-Londons operating within London and each one is largely free to pursue its own planning policy with virtually no regard to what may be happening in a neighbouring borough and certainly no consideration of any wider strategic impact across the whole city. The classic example of the problems this causes is found within London's approach to tall buildings: for years the

60   The planning system's failure to establish a city-wide tall buildings policy has allowed City towers (right) to spread unchecked into traditionally low-rise Shoreditch (left), marking the erosion of London's distinctive neighbourhood culture.

City of Westminster was violently opposed to tall buildings and objected to several such proposals tabled by Southwark and the City of London just next door. Incredibly, to date, London still has no city-wide tall buildings policy (Fig.60).

City-wide oversight of tall buildings and other issues such as transport and strategic planning itself is theoretically supposed to be provided by the Greater London Authority and the Mayor of London, who has the power to 'call in' and potentially refuse schemes of 'strategic importance to London' approved by individual boroughs. But again, this system leads to problems as the 'strategic importance' threshold is only reached by a handful of schemes and, in any case, GLA policy as expressed in the London Plan (the mayor's official development strategy for the city) does not always tally with policies produced by individual boroughs, leaving consultants sometimes caught between two contradictory statutory compliance systems. Equally, the London Plan document has itself proved problematic, revelling in platitudinous aspirations but short on the kind of hard, definitive policy that sets a clear framework for architects and developers to work within, particularly on larger schemes.

Even when London has been invited to consider the prospect of imposing limited constraints on the proliferation of tall buildings in areas of the utmost historic sensitivity, the planning frameworks have consistently refused to do so. This has most famously been the case around the Westminster UNESCO World Heritage Site, where UNESCO has repeatedly called for the imposition of a buffer zone to protect the area's key heritage assets, calls which both the GLA and Westminster City Council have assiduously resisted. The damaging result is now clear for all to see, with the phalanx of towers on Canary Wharf Group's Southbank Place scheme and Northacre's New Scotland Yard redevelopment drawing selfish and unwarranted attention away from the Palace of Westminster and Westminster Abbey respectively just yards away. These represent crass incursions on the setting of iconic heritage landmarks that would be unthinkable in many other European historic cities.

While these incidents comply with London's historic tradition of an organic planning style that is empirical and reactive rather than prescriptive and proactive, the approach has led to some glaring disparities in planning enforcement across the city. For instance, while residential homeowners are subject to all manner of technical restrictions when it comes to domestic house extensions (some of these admittedly stemming from national rather than local policy), canny and opportunistic developers are able to proceed with vast schemes that are sometimes in clear contravention of planning policy simply because that policy has been specifically designed to be open to loose and flexible interpretation. 20 Fenchurch Street in the City of London provides a sobering case in point, to which I will return in Part III.

Another area where London's planning system has a significant impact on the city's character in its regard to heritage. Surprisingly to many foreign visitors, London has no planning tradition of a protected 'Old City' at its centre; old and new buildings are allowed to mix at will. This has advantages in as much as London provides a thrilling and dynamic sense of contrast between old and new that simply does not exist elsewhere. But it does require robust protections to be applied to protect historic buildings and character and this is not always the case. As with the rest of the UK, a listing system operates in London which identifies buildings of special historic value and provides them with additional protections with regard to alteration or demolition. This is fine for individual buildings, but the listing process does not actively take into account a building's external urban setting and what contribution this may make to its historic integrity or vice versa. Essentially, urban character is not subject to the listing process and does not thereby enjoy the same scrutiny and protections that are afforded to individual listed buildings (Fig.61).

61    New tall buildings have carelessly compromised the famous view of St Paul's Cathedral from Fleet Street, an example that represents one of the many recent planning failures that have helped undermine London's character.

Conservation areas attempt to rectify this oversight by identifying areas of special historic quality and providing them with an additional tier of statutory protection. But again, the protection here is often loosely and vaguely enforced, as evidenced by the scores of redevelopment controversies that have occurred within conservation areas across London. These include Renzo Piano's Paddington Pole and Cube, Hall McKnight's plans for King's College London and of course scores of tall buildings across the City of London, virtually all of which is a conservation area. Equally, unlisted buildings within conservation areas can still find themselves vulnerable to the threat of redevelopment or demolition and, when seeking planning permission, there is no compulsion for developers to respect the character of conservation areas that fall outside the jurisdiction of the determining local authority.

It is also important to note where planning has led to historic successes in the protection and enhancement of London's character. The London County Council of 1889 to 1965, successor to the 1855-established Metropolitan Board of Works, was the first metropolitan government in the world and, as such, it quickly proceeded to amass a blistering set of towering planning achievements that not only transformed London into the first 'modern' metropolis, but virtually created much of the public and social infrastructure we see in the capital today. This ranged from social housing provision to public transport. Central government legislation has also occasionally played its part, the 1931 London Squares Preservation Act came at a time when many London squares were under threat from insensitive commercial development and it was seen as pivotal in protecting the delicate historic composition of scores of these squares and thereby preserving a crucial component of London's character.

## SIGNAGE

Signage plays an important semiotic tool in every city and London is no different. In London, signage undertakes many forms and each one says a little something about the city's urban character. One of the oldest forms of signage in London is the hanging shop type and this still plays an important, though regrettably reduced, role in the city today. In medieval times, shop signage was not merely for decoration or advertising – low literacy rates meant that often the only way of communicating what was sold in a shop from the outside was by having some kind of graphical representation of it hanging above or beside the front door, usually in the form of a painting or some kind of logo or symbol. Two notable examples exist to this day. The rotating pole of red and white stripes outside barber shops recalls blood flow and indicates barbers – bringing to mind Sweeny Todd's historic role as barber *surgeon*. Equally, the three hanging gold balls outside pawnbrokers' shops derive from the logo of the Medici family of ancient Lombardy, the inventors of this form of money-lending.

These signs would often be hung on elaborate brackets jutting into the street and in many instances would be minor works of art in themselves providing a unique means of decoratively and graphically mapping the city. They provided sensory stimulation in the form of visual ornament, but they also provided something of an auditory backdrop to city life as the signs creaked and swayed in the wind. And crucially, by extending the building facade into the street just above eye level, they created a greater sense of intimacy and enclosure for pedestrians, elements deeply embedded into London's urban character. Some of the best remaining examples of hanging signage are to be found in the City on minor alleyways like Artillery Passage and on important thoroughfares like, appropriately perhaps, Lombard Street. Sadly, it is a practice that has largely vanished from our modern metropolitan discourse and with it a simple opportunity to more decoratively frame the urban streetscape has been lost. Contemporary revivals of the tradition, such as in Soho's Kingly Court and, unexpectedly, in the City's own One New Change, are always gladly acknowledged (Fig.62).

Another form of signage relates to advertising. London is not Las Vegas or New York, strict planning rules restrict overly gregarious advertising hoardings and, while the world-famous neon screens of Piccadilly Circus may be the largest of their kind in Europe, they

62　Distinctive historic signage has been retained on the City's Lombard Street.

are a somewhat tamer version of Manhattan's Times Square and are scrupulously overseen by Westminster planning officers. But advertising has still found a way to impact London's urban character. It did so surreptitiously on the South Bank's Oxo Tower in the 1920s when strict laws prohibiting advertising on the Thames compelled the architect to incorporate the letters 'OXO' into the tower's structure, now a familiar landmark in an infinite number of river views. More recently Zaha Hadid Architects has designed a digital advertising board for West Kensington, a 26 m (85 ft) high metallic pavilion that is as much a piece of sculptural art as it is a consumerist staple. And Camden's long-established tradition of left-field, countercultural nonconformity is evocatively conveyed in the wealth of burlesque three-dimensional advertising protruding from its high street facades, where a frenzied, multicoloured profusion of giant boots, tattoos and piercings transform the street into a breathless parade of Anglicised Americana (Fig.63).

Finally, London's character is also conveyed through its street signs. The design of London street signs differs from borough to borough and many of them not only say something about the character and identity of that borough but are classic works of art in their own right. Westminster's are the most iconic and the world famous red and black street signs, with their simple sans serif font, were created by design guru Sir Misha Black in the 1960s. Not only are they now a copyrighted design brand,

63　Camden High Street's gregarious, figurative signage reveals London's alternative, nonconformist side.

but they have gone on to represent the city as a whole on millions of tourist souvenir items across the world. Other boroughs seek to convey more specific messages, with the Gothic typeface of Kensington and Chelsea designed to imply heritage and the tree logo incorporated onto Ealing's street signs a reminder of its position as one of London's greenest boroughs. However, despite the illustrative differences between each borough's graphical depiction, there is one important element they all convey. They reinforce the multifaceted and heterogeneous nature of London's character and help underline the individuality and identity of each of its constituent neighbourhoods.

For a discussion of London Underground signage, see 'Transport'.

## SQUARES

Squares are to London what skyscrapers are to New York or canals to Venice; they are the definitive architectural manifestation of its underlying urban character and civic identity. Amidst the immense scale and bustle of the capital, they project an image of civility, intimacy and serenity that is central to London's wider reputation as a global yet human city. Squares are common to virtually every city in the world, they provide a social gathering point as well as an architectural concentration of the ideas of citizenship, communality and commonality that are essential for any urban condition to endure. But in London, due to their sheer number and unique composition, they also form a compact yet powerful expression of London's multiple urban character traits.

There are hundreds of squares in London. In the Royal Borough of Kensington and Chelsea alone, one of London's smallest boroughs, there are over 100. For the purposes of this study, London's squares have been split into five categories: civic squares; regular residential garden squares; irregular residential garden squares; circuses and crescents; and commercial or retail squares. While public space in London is predominately defined by the square it is not exclusively so and there are a range of other hybrid, public space typologies, such as circuses and crescents, that constitute the full compendium of London's public realm. Each typology says something about the character of London and can be used to construct a detailed picture of how and what exactly London's squares and public spaces contribute to the character of the city.

The sections below are also to be read in conjunction with the London Public Space Character Matrix (see Table 2 in the Appendix, pp 152–55). This table attempts to classify the different characteristics of 60 London squares in order to identify their key physical criteria and the frequency with which they occur in the capital. This is useful in constructing an overall picture of which public space features help define the city's urban character. Please note that the examples of squares provided in the categories below and in the matrix are by no means comprehensive and have focused primarily on central London and Canary Wharf in order to draw representative conclusions applicable to the whole of the capital.

## Civic Squares

✦ Bank Junction
✦ Buckingham Palace Rond Point
✦ Covent Garden Piazza
✦ Granary Square
✦ Guildhall Yard
✦ Horse Guards Parade
✦ Hyde Park Corner
✦ King's Cross Square

✦ Leicester Square
✦ Parliament Square
✦ Paternoster Square
✦ Sloane Square
✦ Trafalgar Square
✦ Waterloo Place
✦ Westminster Cathedral Piazza

The civic square is the definitive city or town square, a formal, public gathering place in the manner of an Italian piazza or American plaza. In the European or American model such a space is likely to be paved, but the first clue as to the unique nature of London's equivalents is that they often have green spaces at their centres, as is the case at Leicester Square and, more extensively, Parliament Square. This incursion of natural landscape into an area that would be typically defined as hard paving elsewhere, marks the significance of the role natural landscape plays in the assembly of London's urban fabric and character. Another common feature on, say, the European piazza model is that the spaces are usually formally composed, with identical buildings placed symmetrically on either side of the square with a dominant focal point, such as a monument or fountain, placed at the centre. This inevitably extends from the classical architectural tradition with the central focal point dramatically conveying the idea of a melodramatic baroque climax. Countless European civic squares conform to this arrangement, such as the Place de la Concorde in Paris or the Heldenplatz (Heroes' Square) in Vienna.

But London civic squares rarely embody this formal tradition, preferring instead a more varied array of building colours, styles, facades and geometries converging on a loose, geometrically defined space. This kaleidoscope of irregularity is evident at Bank Junction, Hyde Park Corner, Parliament Square, Paternoster Square and Sloane Square and each case reinforces the tradition of organic informality that strongly informs London's urban character. Horse Guards Parade may be London's largest central space and is encircled by a dramatic sequence of monumental classical buildings, but it is the result of organic, piecemeal

64   London's Trafalgar Square (1830) is one of the world's most famous public spaces.

development over the centuries rather than a fixed urban masterplan.

In fact, if we identify three of the core ingredients of the European civic square tradition as being formal composition, hard paving and a dominant focal centrepiece, then Table 2 shows that only four London squares conform to this rationale: Buckingham Palace Rond Point, Covent Garden Piazza, Granary Square and Trafalgar Square (Fig.64). Moreover, at least three of these examples come with caveats that still assert London's eccentricities even when the square in question is at its most formal: the Rond Point is obviously not a square and is virtually submerged in the middle of a park; Granary Square is only symmetrical on one side and enclosed on two; and the southern side of Trafalgar Square is not only wilfully asymmetrical but features irregular elevational compositions. All these characteristics would probably invite disqualification from consideration as a formal European civic space.

London civic squares do occasionally have moments of monumental formality. Though not technically a square, Waterloo Place is unmatched in London for its compositional symmetry and axial precision, and the arched colonnades and towering central church portico of Covent Garden Piazza probably identify it as London's most convincing attempt at a formal European square. But the tradition of civic spaces in London forms a unique expression of the looseness and informality ingrained into the city's character. One can find no better example of this humanistic aspect to London's civic spaces than watching schoolchildren climb over the stoic bronze lions at Trafalgar Square for, unlike much of the European formal civic square tradition, squares in London tend to invite involvement and engagement rather than demand detachment and awe.

## Residential Garden Squares (Informal/Irregular)

✦ Berkeley Square
✦ Cadogan Square
✦ Charterhouse Square
✦ Chester Square
✦ Golden Square
✦ Gordon Square
✦ Hanover Square
✦ Hans Place
✦ Kensington Square
✦ Lincoln's Inn Fields
✦ Lowndes Square
✦ Manchester Square
✦ Portman Square
✦ Russell Square
✦ St James's Square
✦ Smith Square
✦ Soho Square
✦ Vincent Square

By far the most common square type in London is the residential garden square. Table 2 shows that, of the squares surveyed, well over half are either residential or adapted from residential origins. Unlike the historic prototype of the

European town square or piazza, London's squares are almost overwhelmingly residential rather than civic in origin, a circumstance that is key to understanding the unique model of domesticity London's architecture presents and the historic influence of private enterprise in the assembly of the capital's public realm. Practically all of these squares are a result of private development rather than the monarchy or the state: Table 2 shows that three-quarters of the 60 squares surveyed were developed in this manner, a percentage that would be considerably higher were suburban London, with its significantly lower incidence of civic squares, included. This statistic also provides critical historic context in which to frame the current controversy about privatised 'public' spaces across the city. Privatised public space is not new to London, it has been the mechanism used to deliver the vast majority of the city's public realm for the past 300 years. Most of the squares in this category were developed by aristocratic landowners in the 17th, 18th and 19th centuries and today form part of their modern London property legacies which are collectively known as the Great Estates. Therefore, it is not private ownership that damages the character of public space in London, but the means by which the square is managed, designed, secured and accessed, regardless of ownership.

The physical composition of these garden squares is relatively simple. The square will be encircled by a range of terraces and the garden in the centre will often be surrounded by railings. Historically, the gardens would only have been accessible to the residents of the square, a restriction which is still enforced at a handful of squares such as Cadogan Square, Portman Square and Lowndes Square. But in the vast majority of cases the gardens are now open to the public. The restricted garden access at selected squares remains a sensitive issue and can easily be viewed as a socially regressive consequence of private assembly, one that foreign visitors in particular find extraordinary in the centre of an open, modern city. Nonetheless, in the principle of a speculative property market securing civic embellishment and shared amenity, these squares still reveal the extent to which private sector benevolence, even when conditional, has

65    The variety of frontages, materials and building heights on St James's Square (1662) is typical of many of London's residential garden squares.

made a significant contribution to the historic development of London (Fig.65).

The fact that it is a garden occupying the centre of these squares is obviously yet another conspicuous reassertion of the extent to which the picturesque idyll of natural landscape permeates deep into London's urban character and psyche. Table 2 indicates that two-thirds of the London squares surveyed have soft rather than hard landscaping at their centres, a figure that would verge on the infinitesimal in many comparable European cities. So strongly ingrained is the natural landscape aesthetic that permeates London squares, that even architecture is forced to submit to organic hegemony. The elevations

facing onto many London squares are diverse and irregular, featuring a host of different building heights, colours and materials. Golden Square, Lincoln's Inn Fields, Soho Square and St James's Square provide prime examples. While these squares may have initially been formally planned – for instance, Soho and St James's Squares exhibited far greater uniformity at their inception – the pattern of redevelopment over the centuries has conspired with wartime bombing and loose conservation planning to instil considerable architectural variety and irregularity onto the elevational compositions that encircle the central gardens. But it is undeniable that the pronounced affinity for a picturesque naturalism that eschews regularity and symmetry certainly helped provide subliminal intellectual validation for the piecemeal dismantling of architectural formality that many London garden squares proudly display.

## Residential Garden Squares (Formal/Regular)

- ✦ Bedford Square
- ✦ Belgrave Square
- ✦ Bloomsbury Square
- ✦ Cavendish Square
- ✦ Eaton Square
- ✦ Fitzroy Square
- ✦ Grosvenor Square
- ✦ Tavistock Square
- ✦ Trinity Church Square

Table 2 shows that two-thirds of the squares surveyed are based on an irregular, informal composition. But on a handful of occasions London does bend its garden square template to accommodate formality and the results rarely fail to impress. Grosvenor Square remains one of London's oldest garden squares and, though largely redeveloped from its original Georgian

66   The central accents and consistent rooflines and materials of Bedford Square (1783) identify it as one of London's formal squares.

form with neo-Georgian red-brick ranges, it still retains at least three largely identical sides and easily remains one of London's most monumental public spaces. As London's second-largest square, Belgrave Square is more extensive, so that, with its central garden, its four ranges cannot really be viewed in unison but must be appraised individually. Broadly, many of the features inherent in these two key squares – scale, symmetry, uniformity and monumentality – percolate down to the selection of other London residential squares that embrace this more formal aspect. Bedford Square and Fitzroy Square in particular provide fine examples of a grand yet genteel neoclassicism and, with their historic lamp posts, cast iron railings, entrance door fanlights and softly projecting central accents, they encapsulate the classic image of a typical London square (Fig.66).

Even the more magisterial scale of Grosvenor and Belgrave Squares still manages to say something revealing about London's underlying characteristics. Grosvenor Square was created in conjunction with the development of Mayfair at the start of the 18th century. It was essentially an exercise in aristocratic, residential agglomeration, with ambassadorial London townhouses for the landed gentry effectively concealed behind four identical palace-like frontages. In keeping with the palace conceit, the visual impact of individual entrances was suppressed and the presence of the central elevational accent emphasised, characteristics that largely endure to this day. A century later, Belgravia and Belgrave Square were created and, by this point, potential aristocratic residents were joined, and in many instances outnumbered, by a growing aspirational middle class. For obvious reasons of scale and impact, the template of four palace-like frontages overlooking the square was maintained. But interestingly, in a nod to the romanticism of the picturesque movement that had firmly taken hold by this point, and which was to inform huge swathes of modern London's character, the four ranges are not identical, though they are clearly composed as a uniform set.

Interestingly, despite the retention of the palace frontage template, in order to appeal to a less deferential middle class not necessarily willing to submit to absolutist conformity, individual entrances at Belgrave Square are given much greater emphasis than was the case at Grosvenor Square. The projecting stuccoed porches installed here went on to be replicated thousands of times at terraces throughout Pimlico, Belgravia and Kensington and they have gone on to become enduring symbols of refined London domesticity. But the partial rejection of the 'Every Side a Palace' square arrangement methodology and its replacement with the 'Every Man a King' version says much of the extent to which London's character harnesses architecture as a social leveller and humanises mass urbanism by respecting the integrity and inviolability of the individual.

## Circuses and Crescents

+ Arnold Circus
+ Broadgate Circle
+ Finsbury Circus
+ Oxford Circus
+ Park Crescent
+ Pelham Crescent
+ Piccadilly Circus
+ Royal Crescent
+ Westferry Circus
+ Wilton Crescent

Though geometrically circuses and crescents are clearly not squares, they still largely conform to the same residential patterns inherent throughout London's public spaces in as much as they contain a row of townhouses and overlook a garden enclosure. The circus and crescent were largely introduced to London by John Nash at the start of the 18th century as part of his seminal Via Triumphalis improvements for George IV. They were viewed as a means of softening the axial rigour of straight terraces and appealing to the more naturalistically oblique and opaque tendencies of the then well-established picturesque movement, conceptual roles they still largely maintain to this day. The circus effectively sandwiched two crescents together and, even

though Nash initially planned his famous Park Crescent to be a full circus, London has no terraced residential circus to this day, as Finsbury Circus has now largely been rebuilt as offices.

While London has no residential terraced circuses, it does have one residential circus of huge social and historic significance (Fig.67). Arnold Circus forms the heart of Shoreditch's pioneering

67    John Nash's Park Crescent in Regent's Park (1821) was originally intended as a full circus but remains one of London's most famous Regency crescents.

68    Arup Associates' Broadgate Circle (1987) is the civic epicentre of the City's seminal Broadgate office development.

Boundary Estate of 1899, the world's first council estate. Six curved mansion blocks overlook a raised, planted circular platform formed by debris from the slum rookeries demolished to build the estate. Tree-lined boulevards emanate from the circus and the blocks themselves are handsome, gabled compositions of red brickwork adorned with rendered white dressings. By essentially importing the architectural language of the affluent West End to the poor East End, Arnold Circus conveys the immense civic altruism that London's social housing once bestowed on its urban character.

Ironically, it is in fact the commercial and retail sector where London's most famous circuses are to be found, and Oxford Circus and Piccadilly Circus have become iconic and globally recognised destinations synonymous with popular impressions of the city. Significantly, Oxford Circus is one of London's relatively few symmetrically composed public spaces, with its landmark diagonal pedestrian crossing overlooked by four identical curved neo-baroque retail quadrants.

The circus was revived as an urban motif in the 1980s and 1990s by two totemic commercial redevelopment schemes – Broadgate and Canary Wharf – eager to embed themselves into the urban heritage of the city (Fig.68).

## Commercial/Retail Squares

✦ Cabot Square (Canary Wharf)

✦ Canada Square (Canary Wharf)

✦ Duke of York Square

✦ Exchange Square

✦ Finsbury Avenue Square

✦ Finsbury Square

✦ Montgomery Square (Canary Wharf)

✦ New Street Square

The commercial or retail square is one of London's newest public space typologies. They are often found as part of larger redevelopment projects such as Broadgate and Canary Wharf and, as such, they form an intriguing and relatively rare opportunity to see London's strong public realm tradition reinterpreted by contemporary architecture. The results are often innovative, with architects Bennetts Associates' New Street Square forming a convincing reassessment of a City courtyard in the heart of a new office development fed by a web of pedestrian routes, and with the jazzy strips of pulsating, multicoloured lights embedded between the granite flagstones of Finsbury Avenue Square quite literally electrifying the night-time experience it offers. Opened in 2003, Paul Davis + Partners' Duke of York Square forms a historic alternative to the contemporary retail square model by reopening a site that had been previously inaccessible to the public for more than 200 years, consolidating it and its restored neoclassical buildings within a new retail quarter and public square, the latter being the first public square built within central London for over a century. Regardless of age, Table 2 reveals one aspect that unites all but one of the selected examples above; they are all either fully or part-pedestrianised public spaces. In a city whose character is still undermined in many of its public spaces by forced subjugation to traffic, these new squares provide a rare opportunity to reimagine the public realm as an entirely car-free zone.

## STREETS

Together with London's squares and public spaces, London's streets help construct the full physical and social infrastructure of the capital's public realm. Therefore, as with all cities, streets are crucial in conveying London's sense of urban character and identity as they provide a neat encapsulation of the underlying themes and impulses that help form it. Streets in London frequently follow the same development pattern as its squares and public spaces. There is huge variety, they range from the monumental to the intimate but, as with much of London's character, they are often heavily informed by a strong residential emphasis. Irregularity and informality are often recurring themes and, rather than embracing uniformity in the manner of a Parisian boulevard, there is frequently a rich diversity of colours, materials, styles, proportions and rooflines that all combine with the city's fine grain to create a highly dynamic and fluid urban townscape whose haphazard nature matches the organic sprawl of London's retained medieval street layout.

The absence of a grid plan for London means that streets are rarely straight. They wind, quiver, twist and turn with a wilful energy that violently shatters the conventional unity of a townscape into an infinite number of oblique and staggered views. These frenetic physical patterns also frequently appear to denote some form of latent, underlying, unresolved turmoil, chaos and disorder in London's urban psyche. But chaos invites excitement, turmoil denotes energy and disorder heralds surprise, and it is in this dizzying, bewildering streetscape mix of melodrama and intrigue – and not necessarily in the scale and impact of broad avenues or endless vistas that other capitals may deploy – that the true spirit of London lies.

In contrast, many of London's streets also express the city's natural affinity with rural idioms and, despite London's vast scale, it is often its quiet mews and busy central and suburban high streets that are crucial in enforcing the various village neighbourhood typologies that are overlaid on the city's fabric. Inevitably, part of this typology is a strong natural landscaping tradition and the city's innate picturesque instincts are conveyed through its tree-lined terraced streets and ivy-covered mews streets, all softening characteristics which help humanise the urban condition.

There are several different types of street in London and each one provides a new and different means of interpreting and understanding the city's urban character. The principal classifications are included below along with five representative examples of each type. The examples are by no means exhaustive and focus primarily, though not exclusively, on central London.

## Principal Streets (Informal)

✦ Euston Road
✦ Fleet Street
✦ Lombard Street
✦ Oxford Street
✦ Strand

Most of London's principal streets conform to the informal and irregular typology established by many of its squares and public spaces. These streets are rarely axially straight and usually proceed on crooked or winding paths. Fleet Street and Lombard Street in the City provide some of the best examples of this format, and in the latter's theatrical array of street signs, jutting against the gentle curve of its grand facades, it provides an endearingly picturesque rendition of a typical London main thoroughfare, or at least it would, were its eastward vista not assaulted by the brutal incursion of the 20 Fenchurch Street tower. Also, while the narrow width of Lombard Street is pronounced even for London, it is indicative of the tighter grain of the City of London in comparison to other parts of the capital. Stylistic variety and a rejection of architectural uniformity are other key features of London's informal main thoroughfares and streets, like Oxford Street and the Strand, which offer a rich compendium of architectural styles ranging from contemporary to art deco to neo-Georgian to Edwardian baroque, with all the attendant array of colours, materials, scales and elevational treatments therein (Fig.69).

Physically, Oxford Street also typifies the proportions of many London main roads. It is 26 m (85 ft) wide with a pavement that varies from 6 m (20 ft) to 9 m (29 ft) and is variously occupied by trees, bus stops and benches. Buildings are four to seven storeys high and most of the carriageway accommodates one to two lanes of traffic on either side, considerably narrower than some of the multi-lane avenues of Paris of Barcelona. Despite this, both Oxford Street and, even more acutely, Euston Road exhibit many of the problems that have beset London's public realm in recent years and consistently undermine the humanist sympathies of its urban character. Both streets are car dominated, with pedestrian priority often severely undermined by the emphasis given to traffic-management infrastructure such as signage, traffic lights, bollards and staggered crossings. Pedestrianisation, a touchstone topic within London's public realm, has been consistently proposed and rejected at Oxford Street, highlighting the fractious nature of the divergent interests vying for prominence within London's public realm.

69    The Strand is one of the West End's premier thoroughfares and reveals that architectural variety and informality is a feature of London's major as well as minor streets.

## Principal Streets (Formal)

- ✦ King William Street
- ✦ Pall Mall/St James's Street
- ✦ Regent Street
- ✦ Romney Road, Greenwich
- ✦ Whitehall

With the exception of Regent Street, London's formal streets still exhibit considerably more informality and irregularity than would normally be tolerated in many continental equivalents. In Paris, Haussmann's boulevards were designed with mathematical precision, with the width of the street in direct proportion to the height of the building and a formal design code determining streetscape features such as pavement width, tree position and even the height of railings on the facade. No such guidelines exist in London. Accordingly, as one of London's most formal streets, Whitehall reveals a majestic sweep of monumental stone frontages lined by broad pavements and a high consistency in the use of materials. Moreover, Parliament Street at Whitehall's southern tip is the widest street in the UK. But Whitehall is still crooked, relatively stylistically diverse, offers varying building heights, flabbily defined edges and defiantly dissolves into full-blown terraced domesticity at is northern and southern tips. So even when they are at their most formal and well mannered, London's principal streets still indulge in the insurgent irregularity that is their townscape release valve from the behavioural pressure of homogenised uniformity.

70   The superb Quadrant at Regent Street marks the dramatic spatial culmination of what is arguably London's most architecturally formal and consistent major thoroughfare.

Elements of Whitehall's qualified orderliness are also evident at other London main thoroughfares such as Haymarket, Pall Mall and St James's, although unlike Whitehall, all three are at least arrow straight and the latter two are aligned to the vista-terminating townscape focal points of the National Gallery and St James's Palace. Perhaps Romney Road in Greenwich, which separates the Old Royal Naval College from Queen's House and thereby finds itself at the axial fulcrum of one of Europe's most lavish baroque urban set-pieces, occupies the most classically formal street positioning in the capital.

Regent Street is one of a handful of principal London streets that conforms to a continental model of urban formality. It is wide, primarily straight, with a consistent roofline, arcaded ground floors and thematically uniform Portland stone facades that all subscribe to the same monumental, neo-baroque architectural language. Interestingly it is also treeless, a rare and welcome exercise in landscaping restraint that enhances the impact of its set-piece architecture. The fact that Regent Street was developed and designed as part of a single masterplan, a rare occurrence in London, also goes a long way to explaining its uniform planning. But even here in its glorious Quadrant, unruly London still has the last laugh as Nash cleverly turns the tricky misalignment of two parallel axes created by London's organic layout into one of the Europe's most serene and civilising urban streetscape gestures. The Quadrant shows that, in London, awkwardness can be awe-inspiring (Fig.70).

## London 'Boulevards'

+ Kingsway/Aldwych
+ The Mall
+ Northumberland Avenue
+ Park Lane
+ Victoria Embankment

Technically, London does not possess any boulevards in the strict European sense of the word. Typically, European boulevards are wide, straight, tree-lined avenues with porous, active ground-floor frontages that accommodate animated recreational uses like cafes and restaurants whose seating spills out onto the street. Of course, London offers recurring instances of these individual components, but it is rare to find them converging on a single street. The Mall and Northumberland Avenue, for instance, are straight, wide and tree-lined but the former occupies a park rather than an urban setting and the latter offers largely inactive street frontages. Equally the Victoria Embankment, though broad and tree-lined, is neither straight nor lined with active edges and, while Park Lane exhibits slightly more pedestrian activity, its

tranquillity is severely compromised by the eight-lane arterial carriageway that runs alongside it. There is also a question of scale. Oxford Street, in many ways a typical London thoroughfare, is 26 m (85 ft) wide. Yet, while Broadway in New York is generally about the same width, La Rambla in Barcelona is 57 m (187 ft) and, arguably the world's most famous boulevard, the iconic Champs-Élysées in Paris is a colossal 70 m (230 ft).

It is not merely a question of international one-upmanship, a broad width allows for the installation of the various features that animate the boulevard experience, such as wide pavements, benches, cafe seating, trees and possibly public art and water features. The immersive intimacy and kinetic enclosure that London's generally narrower thoroughfares exude is an important part of the city's urban character. But it does complicate the delivery of the conventional boulevard model. Arguably, the London streets that come closest to this model are Kingsway and the Aldwych, both formally and geometrically laid out at the start of the 20th century in a fit of Edwardian imperialist expansionism and sporadically providing the width, scale, activity and coherence required to support the boulevard typology (Fig.71). Compliance

71   With its wide, tree-lined pavements, formal frontages and axial focal point of Bush House, Kingsway conforms to many of the rules of a typical European boulevard.

with this typology by a subtle rearrangement of carriageway, pavement, planting and ground-floor uses could dramatically enhance a number of other streets such as Park Lane, the southern end of Edgware Road and Euston Road. This could, in turn, provide a uniquely formal and ordered means to enhance the city's urban character by creating a hybrid London boulevard typology that mixes European formality with London's indigenous asymmetric sprawl.

## Terraced Streets

+ Cumberland Terrace
+ Gower Street
+ Millfields Road
+ Roupell Street
+ Westbourne Terrace

Of all the hundreds and thousands of streets in London, it is the terraced street that is arguably the most common. Their format is simple, a line of terraced houses with or without bay windows and with individual or paired front entrances (the Georgians preferred individual, the Victorians paired) will line the street and be separated from the pavement by a defensible strip of private land. The strip will be of varying depth and is normally enclosed behind railings in central London, or by a short wall in outer London, where it is often planted. Occasionally, the strip may be eliminated altogether to allow the building to hug the pavement line, a common utilitarian feature of the more modest terraces built for industrial workers in locations like Greenwich, Lambeth and Bethnal Green. The inclusion of a basement might necessitate a short flight of steps up to the entrance for added gravitas, as is the case of many of the grander central London terraces. The entrance itself is usually expressed as a recessed or projecting porch or sometimes flat against the line of the building.

This simple residential kit of parts can be adapted to suit a multitude of formats which range from the colossal monumentality of the towering stucco terraces that overlook Belgravia and Regent's Park to the ubiquitous Victorian two-storey, pitched roof and bay window terraces that hungrily encroach across the suburban neighbourhoods of outer London. While there is a clear difference in scale, both extremities are linked by a number of typological commonalities that are key to London's character. Both show the mass urban condition broken down into more legible, individually articulated, dwelling house components, a key feature of London's human scale that could not be conveyed through the compartmentalised anonymity of flats or apartment blocks more popular in other cities. Both show how domesticity in its various forms is central to London's civic identity. Both reveal the innate variety of London's townscape and materiality. Both demonstrate the ease with which London's streetscape can potentially adapt to a more naturally landscaped public realm. Both reinforce the city's heritage, a role atmospherically conveyed by forensically preserved terraced streets like Roupell Street and Little Green Street. And both show how individuality, informality and variety – a brightly coloured door here, an overhanging window box there – can be used to soften the grinding geometric rigour of the repetitive assembly of bay after bay after bay of doors, windows and frontages.

In fact, while one thinks of Georgian terraces as richly proportioned and individually detailed, streets like Gower Street reveal almost modernist levels of mechanistic repetition. And herein lies one of the historic paradoxes of London. For it was while he was in exile in London in the 1830s that the future Napoleon III of France would wander around the monumental Regency terraces of Regent's Park and the West End marvelling at how London had managed to manipulate the mundane, metropolitan provision of mass housing into a potent architectural expression of imperial splendour. Thirty years later what he had seen in London helped inspire Baron Haussmann's Herculean Second Empire transformation of Paris into the city of mighty boulevards we see today. Therefore, one of the key international legacies of London's terraced streets is that one of the most unplanned capital cities of all helped inspire one of the most planned (Fig.72).

72    The monumental grandeur of Regency Nash terraces like Carlton House Terrace (1832) was to form a
major influence on Napoleon III's Second Empire reconstruction of Paris 30 years later.

## Minor Streets

✦ Carnaby Street

✦ Downing Street

✦ Great Russell Street

✦ Motcomb Street

✦ Shad Thames

For many, it is away from its main streets and
in the sometimes impenetrable labyrinth of its
minor roads, side streets and backstreets that the
true character of London emerges. Here, like an
unruly schoolboy ripping off his tie as soon as the
school day ends, all the pretence at uniformity
that we see on streets like Regent Street and
Whitehall is gleefully discarded so London can quite
literally revel in the tangled tumult of its jumbled

streetscapes and undisciplined grid. The former
comes in the same mix of diverse colours, materials,
rooflines, styles and proportions we see in many of
the city's public spaces and principal thoroughfares.
Again, these are often channelled through a
notional framework of informality, domesticity and
occasionally, a village-like atmosphere. Additionally,
the added sense of enclosure that the narrower
street widths and more modest scale provides,
intensifies the sense of intimacy and immersion
that many of London's smaller streets offer.
These sensations are emphasised further when
a vibrant and animated mix of ground-floor uses
are introduced, such as the cafes, pubs and retail
outlets that proliferate on streets like Neal's Yard
and Carnaby Street.

The irregular layout of London's minor streets
also provides interesting clues as to where exactly

London's civic priorities lie. London's minor streets may be secondary routes, but they punch significantly above their weight when it comes to their relationship with major buildings and their ensuing impact on London's fabric, layout and identity. In virtually every other major city in the world prestige buildings like the British Museum and the Royal Opera House would take centre stage within the city's plan and probably sit behind large public squares that form the nodal hinge from which other streets and avenues radiate. But in London, these buildings endure the pronounced civic humiliation of being relegated to backstreets simply because London's entrenched organic layout refuses point blank to bend to their will. Even when these buildings are placed on main thoroughfares like the Royal Courts of Justice on the Strand, they are not permitted the courtesy of being set back from the pavement behind a grand entrance forecourt but they must instead, humbly assume their position along with adjacent post offices and pubs right on the same paving line as everyone else.

The priority given to the humble backstreet rather than the grand civic square is yet another example of the humanised domesticity that runs deep in London's character. It also electrifies the experience of walking through London's backstreets; amongst all the residential modesty you might just stumble across a hulking classical temple like Belgravia's Pantechnicon or Mayfair's Royal Institution patiently waiting on the same paving line as all the smaller buildings incongruously huddled on either side of it (Fig.73). In hindsight, even the British Museum should be grateful for its forecourt. Furthermore, it is not by accident that the British Prime Minister resides in an innocuous terraced house on an inconspicuous side street. Not only is this pointed relegation a celebratory political concession to London's streetscape culture, but it also counts as the kind of subversive rejection of authoritarianism that is evident throughout London's history. First and foremost, it marks a perverse contemporary manifestation of what King Charles II discovered to his cost when he tried to implement Wren's post-Great Fire of London rebuilding plan for the City: in London, it is the street and not the set-piece that is sovereign.

73   The surreal contrast between the conventional terraces of Belgravia's Motcomb Street and its monumental Pantechnicon building (1830) reflects the extent to which improbable spontaneity is an energising characteristic of London's side streets.

## High Streets

+ Camden High Street
+ Chiswick High Road
+ Kensington High Street
+ Marylebone High Street
+ Piccadilly

There are around 600 high streets in London and they form the principal retail hubs in the various town centres across the city. They usually conform to a familiar template: an active ground floor marked by a parade of shops offset by either a shopping centre or arcade and often located near civic amenities like a church, library or town hall. On occasion a town square might also be part of the composition. Additionally, as with so much of London, while the ground floor is allocated to retail, the floors above, in character if not in usage, are likely to be residential (Fig.74). Inevitably in central London this arrangement is executed on a grander scale; Piccadilly's concentration of high street amenities not only includes shops and arcades but the Royal Academy, the Ritz Hotel, Green Park and a Wren church, all dressed in architectural finery. But it still largely conforms to the same usage and compositional template found on high streets across the capital. Marylebone High Street provides a more intimate hybrid of the West End and outer London formats but is marked by a palpable village-like feel of communality and intimacy, albeit of the affluent kind. Each high street also tends to give clues as to the wider character of its particular attendant neighbourhood. While Chiswick High Road is leafy and urbane, Camden High Street is subversive and irreverent. The growth of internet shopping, of course, has posed the same threats to London high streets as those across the country and a degree of creative repurposing might be necessary for them to survive in the future.

74  Such is the strength of London's residential character than even high streets, like Hoe Street in Leyton, assume a domestic look.

75   While many of London's street markets are located on unassuming side streets that are largely domestic in character, Leadenhall Market in the City (1881) occupies opulent, purpose-built arcades.

## Street Markets

✦ Leadenhall Market

✦ Portobello Market

✦ Ridley Road Market

✦ Tachbrook Street Market

✦ Walthamstow Market

London's street markets are an intrinsic and sensuous component of its urban character. Sights, smells, sounds and touch all converge to create a very human expression of urban life, so much so that architecture takes something of a back seat to the vibrant urban theatre taking place among the customers, traders and their wares. London's street markets tend to be surrounded by buildings at their most modest and retail at its most domestic.

Sometimes buildings might only be two storeys high and are normally shielded from full view by a canopy of stalls and the bustle of crowds; the very epitome of background architecture. Even when markets, like the world famous one on Portobello Road, find themselves contained within prettily coloured facades, these markets are still a relatively rare example of a public realm where, for once, the public is more important than the realm. This is music to the ears of a city whose humanist empathy is as pronounced as London's, which is one reason why historically, and to this day, street markets have thrived in the capital. Additionally, in the urgency of crowd movement and the concentration of people they contain, London's street markets form a kinetic concentration of the energy and dynamism that permeates its urban character. Inevitably, central London offers grander enclosures in which the markets can trade, and at Leadenhall Market we see a stunning Victorian rendition of Milan's Galleria Vittorio Emanuele II adapted for London use (Fig.75).

## Mews

+ Archery Close
+ Kynance Mews
+ Red Lion Yard
+ Rutland Mews South
+ Wilton Row

Mews display the latent schizophrenia that lingers deep in London's urban character because, for every grand townhouse or palatial terrace in Belgravia or Mayfair, a not-so-dirty little secret lingers behind it. But, unlike Dorian Gray's monstrous picture, this secret is a happy one, for in London's mews we see all the grandeur and formality stripped away and replaced with some of the most idyllic, picturesque and rustic renditions of urban living to be found in any major capital city in the world. London's mews are the domesticated flipside of its grand squares and streets; they provide the opportunity for the city to embrace the village and natural aesthetic that are recurring themes of its urban character at full throttle. In their sheltered intimacy, domestic scale,

76 London's network of mews occupy a secret hinterland of cobbled, planted, narrow courtyards that emphasise the city's domestic character and are often a charming and idyllic refuge from the bustle of its main streets.

cobbled surfaces, snug enclosure, often profuse planting and most importantly in their complete abandonment of uniformity, London's mews provide a momentary opportunity for the city to revel in the tranquil townscape themes that are closest to its heart (Fig.76).

## STYLE

London presents a veritable cornucopia of virtually every principal style of architecture that has been developed over two centuries of Western civilization. While Rome is principally associated with the baroque, Paris with the Beaux-Arts and Second Empire style of Baron Haussmann's endless boulevards, Chicago with the sleek modernism of skyscrapers and Miami with the decadent whirl of art deco, London features representations of all these styles and many, many more. Together they emphasise the sense of variety and diversity that defines London's urban character. London also contains individual neighbourhoods which are synonymous with a particular architectural style. For instance, Westminster's historic centre offers an exemplary cluster of medieval architecture; Bloomsbury is famous for its Georgian terraces; Regent's Park is indelibly linked to its sumptuous range of Regency terraces; contemporary architectural styles resonate at Canary Wharf and at the Queen Elizabeth Olympic Park; and, despite its varied and frenetic cityscape, the City of London is still associated with Gothic churches and baroque architecture, the latter exuberantly conveyed through its incomparable collection of Renaissance churches and surviving Edwardian banking halls.

If one were to identify a single style that comes closest to encapsulating the entirety of the city, it would arguably be classicism. London is clearly not a classical city in the sense of it being based on the kind of ordered, axial and formally arranged urban plan we see in Washington DC, Savannah or Turin. But in terms of sheer number of buildings, it is the classical style and all its manifold subgroups ranging from Palladian to baroque that dominates much of London (Fig.77). Whether analysing principal thoroughfares like Regent Street, Whitehall or the Strand, the side streets of Mayfair or Soho or even the high streets of town centres

77   Though London's baroque period was relatively short-lived, in Christopher Wren's St Paul's Cathedral (1710) it produced one of the world's most famous buildings.

dotted around suburban London, it becomes clear that it is classical architecture that won the hard fought and so-called 'Battle of the Styles' between classicism and Gothic in the mid-19th century. Consequently, notwithstanding the awesome iconic power of the Houses of Parliament, when contemplating the historic character of London, one is probably more likely to subconsciously visualise a pediment, portico or column than a pinnacle, pointed arch or flying buttress.

That said, Gothic and medieval architecture does not come far behind in its encapsulation of London architectural character, and buildings like Westminster Abbey, the aforesaid Palace of Westminster, the Royal Courts of Justice,

St Pancras Station, Tower Bridge, Southwark Cathedral and a host of Gothic and neo-Gothic churches do much to popularise global impressions of an ancient and venerable city. Due to classicism's domination of the London streetscape, it is also momentarily thrilling to see a Gothic style normally applied to ecclesiastical or civic buildings adapted for more rudimentary commercial or office purposes, such as the cusped Venetian pile of 26 Throgmorton Street or the sublime 33–5 Eastcheap, both in the City. Equally, such was the Victorian obsession with medievalism during the Gothic revival that they injected multiple Gothic references into the thousands of terraces they built across London;

features like front doors inset with stained-glass vision panels are Gothic traits now synonymous with London's residential character. Buildings like the Tower of London, Westminster Cathedral, Temple Church, St Bartholomew the Great and the infectiously quirky House of St Barnabas in Soho, forge an even older path, referencing Norman and Romanesque architecture to further underline London's ancient origins. Save for precious fragments of the historic London Wall dotted around the City of London and preserved subterranean relics underneath it, little exists from the Roman or Saxon periods.

Despite being a historic city, modern and contemporary architecture has also done much to define London's urban character. Art deco may only have been sporadically and experimentally embraced in the 1930s and 1940s but it was often realised with spectacular results and did much to acclimatise a hesitant and reluctant city to the modernism that had already firmly established itself in other cities across the world. Fleet Street and Oxford Street became unlikely hubs of the style, with buildings like the former Daily Express and Daily Telegraph headquarters and the House of Fraser and Marks and Spencer Pantheon department stores providing the city's finest examples of the style. Its utilisation on many of the factories of west London and the stations of the then expanding London Underground did much to cement modernity into London's urban lexicon. The Brutalism that followed it after the war was implemented with notably less success, and for decades buildings like the Barbican, Centre Point, the National Theatre, the now-demolished Robin Hood Gardens, as well as scores of other similar mid- and high-rise council estates, were seen as pugilistic, modernist pariahs that had helped to ruin London. The brand rehabilitation that much of this style has undergone in recent years, has led to a new appreciation of the work of modernists like Erno Goldfinger and Denys Lasdun, and monumental works like Neave Brown's Alexandra Road Estate are rightly recognised for their ingenious and pioneering reinterpretation of traditional London residential and architectural themes.

London also offers striking and celebrated examples of contemporary architecture, and some

78  Richard Rogers's landmark Lloyds Building (1986) is an example of the high-tech style of the 1970s and 1980s.

of the foremost architects working in the world today have produced buildings in the capital. These include Zaha Hadid, Renzo Piano, Jean Nouvel, Rafael Viñoly and Frank Gehry. Richard Rogers controversially ushered the high-tech style into London with his still divisive Lloyds Building (Fig.78) of the 1970s and 1980s and has provided softened later versions of the idiom with the Millennium Dome, Leadenhall Building and One Hyde Park blocks of flats. Norman Foster's unique, modernist combination of futuristic experimentation, technological sophistication and industrialised rigour has also bequeathed a number of landmark buildings to London including 30 St Mary Axe (the 'Gherkin'), the Bloomberg Building, the Millennium Bridge and the sublime Great Court at the British Museum.

One of the most conspicuous symbols of contemporary architectural style in London has been the tall building, but its largely unresolved integration into London's historic fabric has proved deeply controversial. While style is a cyclical ingredient of urban character, form tends to be more permanent and failure to integrate tall buildings into a historic fabric can do significantly more harm than the stylistic variations with which London is familiar. The stylistic tension inherent in London's high-rises also begs the broader question of how well the capital can accommodate new and old styles sitting side by side. Contrast is a theme that runs through London's character, but is all contrast legitimate or can insensitive juxtaposition lead to chaos instead? It is a question yet to be resolved but one that is of paramount importance in the coming decades if London's architectural character is to retain any credibility in the 21st century. In terms of architectural style and its impact on character, London's experience is largely positive. The immense stylistic variety of London's buildings proves that as long as new architecture addresses the key themes that run through London's character, such as intimacy, informality, domesticity, materiality, nature, staggered views, historic sensitivity and positive engagement with streetscape and public realm, then the city can accommodate virtually any architectural style there is.

## TOPOGRAPHY

London is situated on a sedimentary basin known as the London Basin, a chalky bedrock which stretches across south-east England from Berkshire to the North Sea. Both London and the Thames Basin are cut in two by the River Thames, London's principal river and the primary geological, topological and, in many ways, psychological nucleus of the city (see 'Waterways'). The basin has had three primary influences on London's character. First, its chalky

subsoil deposits were eventually used to form the brick from which hundreds of thousands of buildings and terraced houses across the city were built, elevating the substance to arguably what is London's definitive building material. Second, until the mid- to late 20th century, chalk was thought to be an inappropriate geological substrate for the construction of tall buildings, one of the many cultural and economic reasons why the American skyscraper boom of the early 20th century failed to make any significant impact in London until well after the Second World War. And third, the basin ensures that London is a relatively flat city whose development has been largely unimpeded by topographical impediments. Equally, with the exception of the footings of the North Downs which creep into the south London boroughs of Croydon and Sutton, London's lack of outlying hill restraints has meant that the city has been able to develop in all directions and assume an approximately circular boundary. This is in contrast to localities like Salt Lake City, whose eastern sprawl is effectively terminated by the spectacular linear ridge of the Wasatch Range.

However, the relatively few hills London does have (none of which are more than a few hundred feet high) have had a notable and dramatic impact on the city's character. North London is defined by a number of these hills, and the steep inclines at Muswell Hill, Alexandra Palace, Hampstead Heath and, to the north-west, Harrow-on-the-Hill offer opportunities for the display of spectacular city panoramas and provide a potent reminder of the extent to which London's park and natural landscapes define the city's built environment and considerably soften and humanise its urban character. Hills like Crystal Palace, Richmond Hill and Shooters Hill execute the same role south of the Thames. These peaks also serve to reinforce the residential nature of suburban London in as much as they display a seemingly endless patchwork of creeping terraced streets woven into the outer environs of the city. Primrose Hill occupies an even shallower summit but due to its proximity to the northern boundary of central London, provides one of London's defining viewpoints and also indicates the alarming extent to which uncoordinated high-rise sprawl has diluted the city's urban character and visual coherence.

79   The gentle incline of historic alleyways like Lovat Lane is a feature of many London streets that wind down towards the River Thames.

Central London itself is relatively free of hills but the emergence of each one provides precious natural opportunities for dramatic urban set-pieces. The City only has three shallow hills – Cornhill, Tower Hill and Ludgate Hill – but it utilises each one to enhance the nature of its underlying character. Cornhill is the shallowest and has also given its name to an important City street. The street is relatively straight for the City's irregular layout, but the gentle curves and misalignments conspire with its gentle slope and narrow width to enhance the winding, picturesque quality of its streetscape (Fig.79). The topographical impact of Tower Hill may be mitigated by its barely perceptible incline from the adjacent River Thames, but the siting of both the Tower of London and Tower Bridge here transform it into one of London's most iconic locations. And St Paul's Cathedral is conspicuously placed atop Ludgate Hill, the City's highest point, in order to disperse its scale and impact across an even larger area than might otherwise have been the case.

One consequence of London's relatively flat terrain has been to elevate any level transfer within its public realm that is negotiated by steps into a rare and potentially dramatic spatial event. This happens in a grand manner with the formal steps at Trafalgar Square, Waterloo Place, King Charles II Street at St James's Park and the South Steps at the Royal Albert Hall (Fig.80). But when steps are deployed to burrow multilevel connections through London's narrow backstreets, they can heighten the sense of intrigue and discovery that the city's irregular layout bestows on its urban character. Some of the best examples of these in central London are Vine Hill, Surrey Steps, Carting Lane, Cockpit Steps, Savoy Buildings and Wardrobe Terrace.

80   Central London's relatively flat terrain ensures that changes in level such as those negotiated by the steps behind the Royal Albert Hall (1871) assume a dramatic presence within the urban streetscape.

## TRANSPORT

Of all world cities, London has arguably been the most successful at turning its various modes of public transport into a potent expression of street architecture, civic identity and urban character. London's red buses are an iconic presence recognised across the world and, to an only slightly lesser degree, its black cabs are also widely synonymous with the city. Even graphical representations like London Underground's famous roundel and Harry Beck's legendary tube map have become global brand logos indelibly linked to London's image and identity. Few other public transportation systems worldwide come close to this level of brand identification, with New York's yellow cabs followed by the Art Nouveau version of the Paris Metro logo arguably the next most prolific examples. But for Londoners, who see their various modes of transport as a prosaic necessity, it is often easy to underestimate or ignore the sheer power they wield in exporting its urban character to a wider global audience.

So how has public transport become such a powerful expression of London's urban character and what can designers learn from it about how character can be concentrated and commoditised in such an endearing and compact way? The first and most obvious explanation is colour, and this applies most obviously to London's red buses. For over a century, London buses have been an unmistakable and ubiquitous component of the city's urban scenography, adding distinctive flashes of colour to the city's physical landscape. Equally, in a city with no discernible formal gateways or entrances, London's buses are often the first sign you have arrived in the capital.

Consistency has also played a role here, and during London's last period of rapid expansion in the 1930s it was fortunate in having a municipal administration and national government that recognised the civic power of visual coordination across the full spectrum of public realm. Virtually the same shade of red applied to London's buses was also carried on postboxes, fire engines and Giles Gilbert Scott's iconic telephone boxes, each incarnation helping form an emblematic, chromatic brand for the city and in many ways for Britain as a whole.

Arguably, the most effective tool in London's public transport arsenal is design. From the angular typeface of its maps and fonts through to the curving Art-deco-esque chassis of its buses and taxis, high-quality design has helped lend architectural credibility to London's transport modes. This is most evident in the iconic Routemaster bus for which, in the same way that Norman Foster once identified the Boeing 747 as his favourite building,[19] there is a strong argument for describing it as one of London's most recognisable buildings. While Thomas Heatherwick's 2012 makeover has come with its technical flaws, it has undoubtedly extended the legacy of these much-loved vehicles for future generations (Fig.81). There are now over 1,000 in Transport for London's fleet;

81 Thomas Heatherwick's New Bus for London (2012) is a contemporary revival of London's iconic Routemaster bus and forms a vibrant, moving part of the city's street architecture.

what other single building could ever hope to have such an invasive and expansive impact on a city's urban character? But even more importantly, the Routemaster succeeds because of how it uses design to characterise the city. For in its subtle dilution of mass transit into a house-sized vehicle complete with bright livery, ergonomic curves and patterned upholstery, it helps soften the urban condition in the same way that London's urban character effectively domesticates and humanises a sprawling megalopolis.

## TREES

London is one of the greenest capital cities in the world. One-third of its land is allocated to public green space[20] and 47 per cent to green space of all kinds, the highest proportion for a city its size in the world. In New York the figure for public green open space is 27 per cent while in Paris it is just 9 per cent. In London there is also 27 sq m (290 sq ft) of green space for every inhabitant while in Istanbul it is 6.4 sq m (69 sq ft), in Tokyo 3 sq m (32 sq ft) and in Buenos Aries just 1.9 sq m (20 sq ft).[21] The most obvious manifestation of trees in most cities is in its parks and London is blessed with some of the most generous and expansive urban parklands of any city in the world. The nucleus comprises eight

Royal Parks, five of which are in central London and form an incomparable ribbon of continuous verdant parkland stretching the 5 km (3 miles) from Notting Hill Gate to Parliament Square.

These parks have their origins as royal hunting grounds bequeathed to the nation from the 17th century onwards and, as such, they frequently retain a more naturalistic and almost rural appearance than the more programmatically defined tradition of urban public parks established in the 19th century and evident at locations like Central Park in New York and Parc Güell in Barcelona. Consequently, at Regent's Park and Hyde Park in particular it is possible to experience rolling fields, wildflower meadows and wooded horizons right in the middle of London, an almost gleeful perversion of the urban condition and a surreal assertion of natural prerogative within a man-made setting. Both of these characteristics are very much unique to London. Furthermore, the naturalistic composition of these parks also provides a vivid reinforcement of the humanistic and informal traits inherent within London's urban character (Fig.82).

As well as these larger parks, London's irregular layout also allows for the insertion of awkward pockets of public garden space woven into the city fabric. Some of the most endearing examples of these are Mount Street Gardens in Mayfair and Postman's Park in the City. These constitute hidden,

82   The view across the lake of St James's Park presents London as a riotous and romantic cluster of domes and spires and heavily emphasises the extent to which the city's natural landscape informs its character.

tranquil green enclaves where leftover urban space has been colonised by nature and projects London's innate capacity for informality, awkwardness and surprise.

While London's parks and gardens show trees located in their natural habitats, they also make a strong contribution to the character of London's streets and public spaces. Streets like Kingsway, the Mall, the Embankment, Birdcage Walk, Constitution Hill, Northumberland Avenue and to a degree, Park Lane, mimic something close to the European model of a tree-lined boulevard, in broad appearance, if not in usage. Equally, long stretches of the banks of the Thames are also lined with trees, another humanising urban gesture that not only reinforces London's natural instincts on its greatest public space, but helps construct a compendium of highly picturesque townscape panoramas of the city. And of course, arguably London's most memorable utilisation of trees and landscaping within an urban setting comes in its great tradition of squares. Whether these are garden residential squares like Belgravia, Bloomsbury or Bedford Square or more civic spaces like Trafalgar, Parliament, or Leicester Squares, it is almost inevitable that trees form part of their visual backdrop and thereby soften and humanise London's urban character and condition.

The strength of this affinity with the natural landscape comes with its drawbacks as well as benefits. When Peter Smithson was designing the (treeless) Economist Building and plaza in St James's in the early 1960s, he observed that 'public space without trees is almost unimaginable in England'.[22] Such is London's regard for the natural environment that it sometimes blurs the boundaries between green space and public space in the city, compromising the tradition and propensity of hard landscaped spaces and encouraging a careless attitude towards the positioning of trees. While London has a strong tradition of public spaces, it does not come in the form of the hard, arid, treeless expanses found in European cities such as Madrid's Plaza Mayor or Siena's Piazza del Campo. This of course helps humanise London's urban condition. But it can also dilute it when trees are sometimes placed haphazardly in inappropriate locations and obstruct set-piece architectural compositions, such as along Aldwych or Whitehall where, until

very recently, the Palladian frontage of the seminal Banqueting House was obscured by the random positioning of a huge London plane tree. Equally, while trees afford the Embankment an indubitable majesty, the blanket of them that obscures the river frontage of Somerset House muddies the clarity of an architectural composition specifically designed to relate directly to the river. Conversely, other stretches of the city that would benefit hugely from the planting of new trees, such as parts of Oxford Street, Euston Road, London Wall and much of the Thames riverside east of Blackfriars Bridge, remain barren. While nobody doubts the hugely positive and humanising contribution trees make to London's urban character, a more rigorous and specific approach to their siting in central London in particular would be very welcome.

## USES

London's relatively informal and organic planning tradition means that areas are rarely deliberately zoned in order to accommodate a specific and prescribed set of uses. Unlike many American or Asian cities, London – and Britain generally – does not employ the term 'central business district' or 'CBD'. This is not because one does not exist in London but because that function is normally a consequence of historic evolution rather than municipal intent conveyed through specific statutory encouragement and protection. Nevertheless, as with every city, over time, certain uses have coalesced around particular areas. London's organic development means these classifications are often very loosely defined. But where they do exist, they still make something of a contribution to the urban character of both the location in question and the city as a whole. Perhaps the one usage type to truly transcend geographic boundaries in London is residential. Housing exists in virtually every area of the city and of all the different classifications and variations of character individual uses bestow, London's residential nature is arguably the defining character trait of the capital (see 'Housing'). But clearly other uses exist, and below is a description of how they affect the character of the constituent part of the city with which they are most strongly associated.

## Academic

The closest London has to an established academic quarter is Bloomsbury, home to the University of London, University College Hospital and the British Museum. The regimental order and proportions of the imposing neoclassical architecture of University College London and the British Museum in particular are highly effective in channelling a heightened sense of academia for the local area, as are the wealth of antiquarian bookshops and galleries that cluster before it (Fig.83). The whitewashed, Gotham-esque hulk of Senate House conveys a similar message, this time via an idiom that speaks of modernist, vaguely totalitarian and somewhat paganistic purity, a characteristic also applicable to the latent occult overtones of the tower of Nicholas Hawksmoor's nearby St George's Bloomsbury church. But it is the order and repetition of the rows and rows of unassuming Georgian terraces in the neighbourhood, several of which are discreetly adapted to house all manner of faculties and institutions, that indicate a local character charged with a sense of studious intellectual propriety. Away from Bloomsbury and evident all across London, the Victorian Board Schools, with their Dutch gables, large windows and buff or red brickwork, provided a newer and less elitist model of urban learning that fused institutional and residential characters into one.

83   Foster + Partners' seminal Great Court at the British Museum (2000) marked a superlative update to London's academic campus at Bloomsbury.

## Offices and Financial

London's primary financial centre is the City of London, London's oldest district and the part most typologically consistent with the international 'central business district' terminology. Today it presents a confusing and chaotic mix of new and old with classical banking temples awkwardly cast at the foot of an increasingly impermeable phalanx of glass towers. Canary Wharf is its contemporary successor and, even though it offers a less arresting and more monocultural urban experience than the City, it is based on an infinitely clearer and more coherent urban plan, namely that of an American downtown-inspired district defined by a series of glass skyscrapers rationally arranged on an orthogonal urban grid. Both districts house negligible residential populations, a demographic curiosity in the capital that has enabled a unilaterally corporate and financial character to take centre stage.

## Culture

Of the top 20 most visited museums in the world, London has six, a higher quota than any other city.[23] Of these, half – the Victoria and Albert Museum, the Science Museum and the Natural History Museum – are in South Kensington, bestowing preeminent cultural quarter status on this urbane district. This reputation is bolstered by the presence of many other academic and cultural institutions including the Royal Albert Hall, the Royal College of Music and Imperial College. Most of these buildings were built in the late Victorian or Edwardian period using terracotta or red brickwork and the highly formalised, monumental aspect given to their architecture plays a key role in constructing the scholarly character of the neighbourhood. Alternately, the South Bank forms Europe's largest arts centre but exudes an entirely different, less formal and more egalitarian character. This is not necessarily channelled through its defining Brutalist architecture, but more through the animation and expansiveness of its incomparable riverside promenade and the enduring spirt of progress and hope its post-war heritage, as the site of the 1951 Festival of Britain, confers. Architecturally, these sentiments are most effectively conveyed through the whitewashed libertarian openness of the Royal Festival Hall. Yet at the opposite end of the scale, the converted warehouses and requisitioned railway arches of Shoreditch and Hackney embody a de-institutionalised and fiercely nonconformist form of countercultural artistic enterprise that, at Hackney Wick, has combined with a highly lucrative application of gentrified dilapidation to turn a formerly deprived, post-industrial backwater into the home of Europe's largest concentration of artists.[24]

## Diplomatic

Most embassies and diplomatic missions in London are clustered in the aristocratic enclaves of Mayfair and Belgravia, London's two most exclusive districts. The mix of palatial townhouses, grand squares and refined classical architecture the districts offer has proved a seductive package for scores of foreign consulates wishing to exert presence and prestige in the most reputable permutation possible of London's indigenous terrace and square typology.

## Entertainment and Recreation

While obviously pubs, restaurants, cafes, bars, clubs, theatres and cinemas are dispersed across the city, their premier hub, by a considerable margin, is the West End. Though outlying central districts such as Shoreditch, Farringdon and London Bridge offer a high concentration of all but the latter two of these activities, it is the West End districts of Soho and Covent Garden where London's most intense recreational concentration lies. As with most of central London, both areas began life as residential speculations but both have proved successful at retaining their historic character while adapting their building stock to a whole range of dynamic leisure or retail-related uses. As a result, this part of London maintains almost 24-hour activity and finds its architecture complimented with a host of neon and illuminated features that electrify the urban landscape at night.

## Government

Westminster and Whitehall form the epicentre of British political life. The iconic landmarks of Westminster, namely Parliament and Big Ben, form the seat of government and are some of the most recognised architectural structures in the world. Their Gothic style conspires with that of the adjacent Westminster Abbey, Westminster School and The Supreme Court of the United Kingdom to form London's most complete rendition of a Gothic or medieval quarter. The broad, staggered sweep of Whitehall comprises a monumental sequence of civil service buildings and attendant statuary whose pomp, in true London understated style, is punctured by the almost comically understated domestic intrusion of Downing Street and the modest yet world-famous townhouse that is the home of the British prime minister. This forms an apt reminder that even when London is at its grandest, its core residential genes are never too far away.

## Hotels

While hotels are obviously spread across the city, the highest concentration of hotels is to be found serving its highest concentration of tourists in central London. Large hotels are scattered across the centre of the city but it says much about London's innate domesticity and modesty that one of the most prestigious, Claridge's, does not overlook a grand urban square as with the Ritz on the Place Vendôme in Paris, but is instead located on a relatively quiet residential side street. The highest concentration of luxury hotels is to be found on Park Lane running alongside Hyde Park, where a series of sumptuous and now sadly demolished mansions have given their name to the row of modern hotels that replaced them. Unfortunately, the opportunity to recalibrate the character of Park Lane as a leafy urban boulevard anchored by its sweep of majestic hotels and prime park setting is utterly wasted by the multi-lane juggernaut of a road that severs one side of Park Lane from the other. Regrettably, this kind of punitive traffic-led misappropriation of the public realm does much damage to London's civilised character at multiple locations across the city.

## Industrial

While parts of west London became synonymous with manufacturing in the 20th century, historically the vast majority of London's industrial output took place away from central London and was primarily focused in east London and the East End. Following mid-20th-century industrial decline, many of these locations became touchstone regeneration projects and the two biggest, Docklands and the Queen Elizabeth Olympic Park, now offer totemic statements on how London's cultural nexus has shifted eastwards in recent decades and on how, as an urban brand at least, the character of east London has evolved from industrial decline to edgy cosmopolitan creativity and chic. Ironically, it is often the same buildings that conveyed both impressions and east London offers a wealth of solid, muscular brick warehouse buildings whose conversion into residential or studio use is now frequently seen as either the pinnacle of modish desirability or the noxious manifestation of gentrified exclusivity. Smaller, light industrial versions of these warehouse buildings exist in central London too and, while they are an integral part of outlying central districts like Shoreditch and Clerkenwell, they always add a surprising utilitarian rigour to London's character when they are uncovered in more unlikely locations like Westminster and Covent Garden, even loitering discreetly just a few feet away from St Paul's. In west London, the Great West Road is sometimes referred to as the Golden Mile due to its incomparable collection of stellar art deco warehouses and factories, many of which have now been converted to residential, retail or commercial use.

## Legal

The Inns of Court form the ancient epicentre of legal life in London. Hidden away from London's main streets and landmarks, the ancient City institutions provide for the accommodation, protection and supervision of barristers in a mesmerising and utterly breathtaking stage-set of Tudor, Elizabethan and classical buildings which forms what is arguably the best-preserved example of medieval London still in existence today. Woven between the buildings is an extraordinary ribbon of sheltered lawns, squares and courtyards that dramatically evokes the strong natural aspect ingrained into London's urban character and also reveals the extent to which that character is charged by the principles of residential intimacy, informality and enclosure.

## Religious

Religion has played an enormous role in the formation of London's urban character; St Paul's Cathedral and Westminster Abbey, provides at least two of its most iconic landmarks. While London is inevitably more secular today than it has been in the past, the peal of church bells still forms one of the most familiar soundtracks of the city. Today the City of London's uncompromising corporate trajectory is such that it is sometimes easy to forget that it is a major religious centre as well as a financial one. As well as the obvious presence of St Paul's, the City has the UK's highest concentration of churches, most of which constitute Europe's finest collection of baroque churches outside Rome. The majority of these City churches were designed by Sir Christopher Wren and, in their extraordinary versatility of design and their innovative deployment of the decorated steeple as a vertical urban landmark, not only did they establish for the first time the (largely unrealised) idea of London as a formal baroque city but they also set the compositional framework that was to define much of London's skyline and townscape character for the next 300 years. Rather oddly, the guild, rather than parish, status enjoyed by many of these City churches means that, in yet another quizzical London contradiction, the vast majority of them are closed on Sundays.

As in so many aspects of London life and heritage, the City's ideological twin is Westminster and, as home to Anglican Westminster Abbey, Catholic Westminster Cathedral and Methodist Central Hall, Westminster effectively forms the spiritual seat for three of the UK's biggest Christian denominations. Inevitably, this liturgical role seeps into the district's urban character which, with its cloistered yards and Gothic spires, provides a romantically charged architectural projection of both ecclesiastical power and contemplative repose. Outside central London, churches still assume the role of ubiquitous urban landmarks and, at locations like Liverpool Grove in Walworth and Trinity Street in Borough, they form the focal point for set-piece neoclassical residential developments in the same way that a supermarket or school now forms the secular anchor for their contemporary equivalents. Equally, in Renzo Piano's adoption of a church spire as the conceptual inspiration for his Shard, we see the enduringly powerful and potent hold that London's religious imagery still has over the development of the city today.

## Retail

Central London, and the West End in particular, remains by far the UK's largest and most profitable shopping destination and, with almost a quarter of a billion visitors a year, Oxford Street is the busiest shopping street in Europe.[25] After residential, therefore, retail is arguably central London's most prolific usage characteristic. The eclectic mix of architectural styles on Oxford Street itself provides an accurate metaphor for the multiple character traits London's retail environment tends to emit (Fig.84). For instance, Regent Street conveys retail exclusivity through a highly formal and forensically configured architectural environment defined by a series of monumental classical facades and a controlled level of elevational conformity and precision that is rare in London. Yet many London high streets outside the centre of the city are expressed by a continuous series of residential facades on their upper storeys beneath which unfurls an almost anomalous parade of ground-floor shopfronts. This arrangement yet again reinforces the strength and informality of London's residential character, as does London's long and colourful tradition of street markets.

84　Daniel Burnham's colossal Selfridges department store (1909) is one of the retail highlights of Oxford Street, Europe's busiest shopping thoroughfare.

## Royal

The triangular district between Buckingham Palace, Trafalgar Square and Parliament Square sees London transformed into a lavish civic stage-set for the ritual of royal ceremonial pageantry and display. It is therefore no accident that the layout of this part of the city sees London at its most formal and axially composed, with palaces and monuments terminating plunging vistas around which buildings are arranged in forensic symmetrical order. The architecture too exudes grandeur and ostentation with the sumptuous renditions of Edwardian baroque applied to Admiralty Arch, Admiralty House, the Queen Victoria Memorial and the east front of Buckingham Palace vying with the stunning neoclassical ranges of Lancaster House, Carlton House Terrace and Waterloo Place, the latter two employing a level of formal compositional planning unmatched anywhere else in London. And with a level of paradoxical conceit that is typical of London, this most architecturally formal of districts is cast against a verdant park backdrop whose stirring picturesque scenery provides one of London's most powerful demonstrations of the extent to which the city's natural landscape informs, enlivens and humanises the character and setting of its built environment. The result, complete with red-carpet tarmac applied to the Mall and colourful crowns encrusted atop lamp posts and flagpoles, is a part of London where the sense of theatricality and melodrama is a palpable and electrifying component of its urban character.

## Sports

The city's three most iconic sporting venues from a global perspective are Wembley Stadium, the All England Lawn Tennis Club at Wimbledon and the Queen Elizabeth Olympic Park, and the setting of each one has a different message to convey about London's character. Wembley Stadium sits in a part of north-west London that was developed as a result of suburban expansion and is situated in a former industrial zone that is currently undergoing massive mixed-use development. Situated just yards from a major retail town centre and within the proximity of terraced and semi-detached housing, Wembley presents an exaggerated version of the stirring, yet jarring juxtaposition of scale and massing that occurs throughout London's residential fabric whenever a large football stadium is placed abruptly within it, a pattern evident from the 9000-capacity Leyton Orient stadium in east London to the new 62,000-seater Tottenham Hotspur stadium in north London. The shift in scale and function is more subtly handled at Wimbledon, where the All England Club's green arena roofs and planted walls integrate themselves seamlessly into one of London's most potent and picturesque village-like contexts. The Queen Elizabeth Olympic Park presents a classic treatise in regeneration, with the former post-industrial wasteland on which it once stood transformed into a vibrant public park which, as with much of London, performs a rich natural backdrop to the built environment, here primarily composed of a series of strikingly contemporary retained Olympic sports venues.

## VIEWS

City views may only provide a concentrated snapshot of the urban townscape but, like photographs, they are immensely useful in constructing a broad visual impression of a physical condition. They are also important therefore, in helping to define urban character by presenting a prescribed set of urban images which, when taken as a whole, are crucial in helping establish and express place and identity. London's informal and organic layout also means that its views follow similar patterns. Landmarks often emerge suddenly in glimpses rather than formal climaxes, a visual affectation that underlines the spontaneity and irregularity inherent within London's urban character.

The setting of major landmarks such as St Paul's Cathedral outlines this point. When approaching St Paul's from Fleet Street the great dome constantly leaps mischievously in and out of view, its jagged approach the topographical and townscape consequence of the winding street line, the rising profile of Ludgate Hill and the staggered rooflines of neighbouring buildings. For the most part, therefore, St Paul's is viewed in oblique glimpses rather than a whole, a unique dilution of scale and monumentality that fits in perfectly with London's humanistic instincts. There are some moments in London's urban landscape when formal views are on offer. The manner in which both Buckingham Palace and Admiralty Arch terminate each end of the long vistas along the Mall and the way in which Bush House forms the axial focal point to Kingsway are two memorable examples, rendered all the more thrilling by the relatively scarcity of this kind of arrangement within London's landscape. But in the main, views in London are a furtive exercise in concealment and revelation and are symptomatic of the character of a city that does not thrust its finery to the forefront but demands that the viewer immerse themselves into its fabric and unpeel it layer by layer like a giant maniacal onion.

Inevitably, in a city with such a strong regard for natural landscapes, views are often framed by nature. Trees are a ubiquitous presence within London's urban environment and, despite London's scale and frenzy, they express the city's picturesque tradition and act as a softening agent to its hard urban form. One of the best examples of this is the view from the bridge across St James's Park lake. To one side, Buckingham Palace appears not as the monumental climax to a grand civic set-piece, but as a formal frontage now only glimpsed between rich green curtains

85    The inconsistency of the London View Management Framework is indicated by the fact that on one side of a City roof terrace even the height of seating is restricted to preserve views . . .

of surrounding trees and natural landscaping. From the other side of the bridge, a fantastic orgy of domes, spires and turrets rises dreamily from Whitehall and is enclosed between unfurling horizons of greenery set above the glistening pool of the lake. It is an irresistibly romanticised and picturesque view of London but, idealised as it may be, it displays how views in and of the city are constantly informed by the ubiquity of the natural world.

Another bridge reveals a different underlying theme of London's urban character: contrast. At 366 m (1200 ft) long Waterloo Bridge straddles the majestic curve of King's Reach, the widest point of the Thames in central London. Crossing Waterloo Bridge inevitably forces Londoners and visitors alike

to make a key topographical choice, either to look east towards St Paul's and the crowded silhouette of skyscrapers in the City that increasingly encroach upon it, or to look west towards Westminster and marvel at the Gothic pinnacles, towers and spires that crowd around Big Ben and Westminster Abbey. Both views encapsulate highly contrasting impressions of London, and the fact that both are attainable from the same location goes to the heart of the dynamic and multifarious nature of London's urban character.

While it would be impossible to protect all views in a city, despite its tradition of informal, organic planning, London makes an attempt to afford special statutory protection to identified strategic views and, by extension, the role they

86   . . . while on the other side a glut of skyscrapers is allowed to proceed unchecked.

play in helping formulate the city's character (Fig.85). The definitive statutory regulation dealing with protected views in London is known as the London View Management Framework, formerly termed St Paul's Heights since its inception in 1937. The framework identifies 13 invisible protected viewing corridors that overlap the city and protect key views of St Paul's Cathedral, the Houses of Parliament and Tower Bridge. But the gradual erosion of these corridors that began in the 2000s, as well as the fact that they afford no protection to other key views in the city (such as the aforesaid St James's Park bridge and Fleet Street to St Paul's sequence), means that the LVMF is increasingly ill-equipped to deal with the threats to London's character (Fig.86).

## WATERWAYS

Of all London's myriad of docks, rivers, channels and canals, one emerges as unassailably preeminent: the River Thames. The Thames is one of the world's great urban rivers and is arguably London's principal public landmark. The UK's second longest river is a defining feature of London's urban character, its great central London stretch forming the majestic foreground to some of the capital's most enduring cityscape images and landmarks. Unlike the Seine in Paris, the Thames is tidal for the vast majority of its path in the city, casting a surging, restless and at times unpredictable avatar of the natural world right into the heart of the urban city.

The true extent of the Thames's natural characteristics is both surprising and significant. Tidal flows can rise and fall by up to 7 m (23 ft) a day and the river is 265 m (869 ft) wide at London Bridge and 448 m (1470 ft) wide at Woolwich, making the Thames one of the widest urban rivers of any capital city in Europe. By comparison, both Moscow's Moskva River and Budapest's Danube measure approximately 200 m (656 ft) wide in the centre of their respective cities, the Seine in Paris is approximately 160 m (525 ft) wide beside the Louvre, Rome's Tiber is 110 m (361 ft) wide at its closest point to Vatican City and Dublin's River Liffey is only 45 m (148 ft) wide at O'Connell Bridge. Therefore, the commanding scale and broad sweep of the Thames injects a palpable sense of confidence, majesty and strength into London's character and the river runs deep into London's subconscious impression of itself as a global seat of power and prestige.

It is not by accident that the mythical figure of Old Father Thames is frequently depicted in art and sculpture as a virile Herculean deity, a wise and bearded oracle whose physical strength is a potent temporal affirmation of absolute symbiotic harmony with the natural world. And yet, for all the majesty and grandeur of the Thames, the organic nature of this natural world still makes itself felt by the relentlessly meandering path the Thames cuts through the city, twisting and turning through the capital like an endlessly quivering whip. This irregularity not only reflects the layout and wider character of the city, but it also casts a series of majestic curving vistas right into London's cityscape, such as King's Reach at Westminster and the Isle of Dogs. This duality of the Thames, its physical strength and its natural instincts, means that of all locations in London, the Thames is where one can feel closest to the city and, conversely, furthest away from it; a glorious contradiction that typifies London.

Along its central London stretch the Thames is lined with various civic and cultural buildings, by far the most famous of which is the Palace of Westminster but which also includes significant London landmarks like Tate Modern, Somerset House, the former County Hall, the More London commercial development and the various arts venues of the South Bank. On the southern side a continuous public promenade runs along the South Bank and much of Bankside in central London, providing an unravelling sequence of spectacular views. A public riverside route also straddles much of the northern side too, the highlight of which is the regal tree-lined arc of the Embankment. Also, while pockets of inaccessibility remain in the City, much has been done in recent years to open up formerly private or industrial river frontages for pedestrian use (Fig.87).

The Thames is spanned by a number of bridges, the highest concentration of which lies in central London. Famously, and inconveniently, there are no London bridges east of Tower Bridge, an appalling historic disparity between east and west London that is an obstructive, though once necessary by-product of the former teeming industrial roles once enjoyed by the Pool of London and Port of London towards the east of the City. Unlike bridges in Paris or Prague, London's bridges tend to lean towards function and utility rather than overt ornamentation. Of course, the one glaring exception to this rule is Tower Bridge, one of the most famous bridges in the world and an iconic symbol of London whose medieval appearance conspires with the adjacent Tower of London to fortify international impressions of an ancient and venerable city. Other more decorative offerings include the cool sculptural purity of Waterloo Bridge, the pinnacled Gothic piers of Hammersmith Bridge and the lavishly illuminated Albert Bridge.

For a city as old as London, most of its bridges are remarkably young, with the oldest, Richmond Bridge, dating from only 1776. This is in stark contrast to other historic European cities; Florence's famous Ponte Vecchio, for example, dates from 1345. Most of London's bridges date from an explosion of bridge-building in the 19th century, when the Corporation of London finally relaxed protectionist bylaws that had maintained London Bridge as the Thames's only bridge crossing for almost 1700 years. Architecturally, the bland modern flyover that is London Bridge is one of London's least memorable bridges. However, as the subject matter of what is arguably the world's most famous nursey rhyme, its current incarnation enjoys unwarranted iconic status. The sale of Old London Bridge to an American entrepreneur in 1968 is also a chastening reminder of the sheer commercial

87 Significant stretches of London's canals have been rejuvenated in recent years and in summer months the Regent's Canal at King's Cross Central is often the backdrop to large public entertainments and events.

ruthlessness that underpins London's urban character and variously threatens the setting if not the fabric of other cherished national monuments.

The Thames today is a busy river, crammed with sightseeing and party boats and now host to a number of popular private commuter riverbus services. But it is no longer an industrial river, and remains a far cry from its heyday in the 19th century when the Pool of London, the stretch of river between Tower and London Bridges, was allegedly so crowded that you could walk across the Thames by stepping from ship to ship. Industrial heritage has left its legacy on the Thames in the wealth of former wharves and warehouses that still face the river, particularly to the east. Many of these, such as at Shad Thames, have been converted for residential use and intermingle with new riverside residential developments. But others, such as Hay's Galleria and Gabriel's Wharf, have been redeveloped for retail and recreational amenities. One positive consequence of the deindustrialisation of the Thames has been the environment. Its brown hue is the result of mud not pollution and, despite it once being a repository of sewage, disease and contamination, today it is widely regarded as one

of the cleanest rivers to flow through a major city in the world. Additionally, the Thames in west London retains a completely different appearance to the industrial character still largely maintained in east London. West of Hammersmith, London's urban fabric slips quietly away and the eventually non-tidal river meanders gently through the kind of picturesque, pastoral landscapes that would not look out of place in the countryside of Devon or Oxfordshire. In its industrial east and picturesque west, the Thames represents the two contradictory extremes of London's character.

As well as the Thames, a number of its smaller tributaries also flow through the capital. The River Lea in east London is one of the longest of these and, by flowing through the regenerated post-industrial neighbourhoods of Bow and Hackney Wick, as well as the picturesque marinas and wide open fields of Walthamstow Marshes and the Lea Valley, it too underlines the extremities of London's character by mimicking the contradictory riparian landscapes of the Thames.

Intriguingly, London is also home to a number of lost rivers, once major waterways that have now been buried deep underground due to centuries of either redevelopment or appropriation as sewers

88   With moored houseboats and riverside cafes, Little Venice captures residential London at its most idyllic and picturesque.

during the Victorian age. Many of these, such as Walbrook, Westbourne and Tyburn, have now lent their names to streets or neighbourhoods. Arguably the most famous is the River Fleet, which flows from Blackfriars Bridge to Highgate and whose rushing stream can still be heard underground through pavement grills around Blackfriars Station. These lost rivers provide a surreal and endearingly folkloric reminder of the ubiquity of the natural world even in the character of modern London. And in the case of the Fleet they also provide a source of inspiration for urban redevelopment. Much of the Fleet runs under the path of Farringdon Road, where heavy wartime bombing and insensitive current and post-war rebuilding ensures its status as, for the most part, a vapid, anodyne urban canyon. Its charisma could be significantly enhanced by the opening up of the River Fleet underneath it in a similar way to the uncovering of the Åboulevarden section of the Aarhus River in Denmark's second city, a move that has been a resounding success.

London's man-made waterways also make a significant contribution to the city's urban character. In the 19th century east London's docks, collectively known as the Port of London, were the largest docks in the world and their closure, which largely took place in the mid-20th century, had a catastrophic effect on the economic and social fabric of the East End. However, their regeneration from the 1980s onwards has been an astonishing success story, with Canary Wharf and the neighbouring wharves and quays of the Isle of Dogs transformed into new urban settlements all strongly defined by their distinctive waterside character.

London also has two principal canals that form a wide arc over much of the northern section of central London. Regent's Canal runs from Limehouse Basin to Paddington Basin while the main section of the much longer Grand Union Canal runs from Paddington to Birmingham. The confluence between the basin and the two canals is known as Little Venice which, with its colourful houseboats and waterside bars and restaurants all primarily overlooked by tree-lined boulevards of grand stucco terraces, presents an idealised and powerfully picturesque waterside variant of London's residential character upgraded to the most tranquil, idyllic and idealised state possible (Fig.88). Pockets of similar, smaller enclaves exist at other locations along the Grand Union and Regent's Canals and, in the canals' car-free edges and their compact dissemination of the alternating residential and industrial townscapes found throughout London, they effectively present a miniaturised, calmer and more intimate simulation of the Thames.

# Part III
# Enhancing London's Urban Character

89　22 Bishopsgate glimpsed from beside London Bridge.

# Projects that Harm London's Urban Character

The 'harm' and 'benefit' entries for each case study refer to the components of London's character identified in Part II of this volume that are relevant to the featured scheme.

+ 5 Broadgate
+ 20 Fenchurch Street
+ 22 Bishopsgate
+ Chapter Spitalfields
+ ME London Hotel
+ Nine Elms
+ Nova Victoria
+ One New Change

## 5 BROADGATE, CITY OF LONDON

+ **Architect:** Make
+ **Client:** British Land
+ **Type:** Office
+ **Completion:** 2015
+ **Harm:** Climate, Colour, Height, Materials, Planning, Squares, Views

5 Broadgate proves that it is not just tall buildings that are capable of wreaking harm on the City of London's character. Until the creation of Canary Wharf in the 1990s, Broadgate was the biggest modern financial campus in London. Even today its 13-hectare (32-acre) site still claims to be the largest pedestrianised neighbourhood in the capital. Broadgate began life in the late 1980s as a commercial development with a difference. An early beneficiary of the controversial 'air-rights'

policy which allowed the space above train tracks at major termini to be sold for commercial redevelopment, Broadgate turned the area above and around Liverpool Street Station into a landmark new financial district. But even more significantly, it transformed the thinking behind office development at the time. Instead of focusing solely on the individual commercial building, Broadgate wove an exemplary series of pedestrianised public spaces between its offices, cleverly ensuring that the scheme not only had a strong civic identity of its own, but was also effortlessly inserted into the public realm and historic fabric that surrounded it. Sheathed in postmodernist uniform, the buildings themselves were of high quality and were created by a stellar assortment of modernist architects including Arup, Peter Foggo and SOM. Crucially, in terms of scale, materiality and proportions, the new office buildings were intrinsically and individually linked to their attendant streets and squares, so much so, that Broadgate's architecture and urbanism formed a unified and coherent whole where the sum mattered significantly more than the individual parts. Broadgate's urbane template not only revolutionised commercial regeneration but it proved to have a huge influence on similar office-led redevelopment projects like Canary Wharf, Birmingham's Brindleyplace and Manchester's Spinningfields. Even today it stands as one of London's defining civic projects of the late 20th century.

This is why the addition of 5 Broadgate defies all possible logic. The new building sits on Broadgate Circle, an extraordinary multilevel rotunda that forms the focal public space within the entire development and is perhaps unlike any other public space in London. The new building also required the contentious demolition of 4 and 6 Broadgate, two blocks which sat on either side of the central axial route that radiated out of the circle to the north. Now both route and buildings have been permanently flattened to make way for by the behemoth that is 5 Broadgate, which now savagely terminates the northern edge of the circle quite literally like an 80 m (262 ft) high steel wall. At 13 storeys, it is almost twice as high as many of its neighbouring blocks and it thereby seriously disrupts the consistency of the carefully constructed townscape roofline the original masterplan established. More disruption is levied by its external cladding, a gaudy stainless-steel casing that is utterly at odds with the darker tones of red stone and bronze panelling that tend to dominate the estate (Fig.90).

Worse, perhaps, is its massing and elevational articulation. The building is depicted as a sterile rectangular fortress with sheer, relentless 12-storey cliff-edge walls plunging down each side. Almost in recognition of an otherwise tedious facade, a series of cuts are made into the external envelope to form windows, primarily an assortment of narrow vertical and horizontal slits and, at a number of stages, a calamitous cross-stich of diagonal incisions. With windows kept to a minimum, feeble attempts are made to puncture the solidity of the block in the form of two large recesses pressed into its upper storeys. But these do nothing to ameliorate the oppressive bulk of this building and, together with its plasticky silver coating, they give the distinct impression of an unsuspecting Broadgate Circle being set upon by the gargantuan rear end of a marauding microwave.

90   5 Broadgate acts as gigantic steel barrier within the once-celebrated Broadgate Estate.

The architects justify the scheme by claiming that its overtly solid envelope is a technological reaction against the environmental inefficiencies of the traditional glass office block and helps minimise solar gain and thereby reduce reliance on internal mechanical ventilation. Equally, they also justify the building's colossal size, 65,300 sq m (703,000 sq ft), as simply being the amount of space occupier UBS required. But urban character cannot be unilaterally determined by sustainability and floorplates and while 5 Broadgate may satisfy environmental and commercial concerns, it has done so by destroying the character, clarity and coherence of a benchmark piece of modern urban design. Sadly, it is not alone in doing so. Barely 15 years after its completion virtually all of Broadgate is now under threat, most of which being conveniently unlisted. Accordingly, similarly insensitive plans to remodel or replace 1–4 Broadgate, 3 Broadgate, 8–12 Broadgate, 2 and 3 Finsbury Avenue Square and 100 Liverpool Street are all underway, each scheme marking yet another irreversible evisceration of what was once an inspiringly symphonic urban narrative.

## 20 FENCHURCH STREET, CITY OF LONDON

+ **Architect:** Rafael Viñoly
+ **Client:** Canary Wharf Group
+ **Type:** Office
+ **Completion:** 2014
+ **Harm:** Alleyways, Climate, Entrances, Height, Planning, Streets, Views

Buildings rarely come more controversial than 20 Fenchurch Street, popularly nicknamed the 'Walkie Talkie'. The notorious 38-storey skyscraper has become a byword for planning harm, appalling contextual insensitivity and, to put it simply, bad architecture. Combined with its prominent location in London's most historic district and the role it plays in destabilising London's already chaotic skyline, then you have all the ingredients for a totemic work of architecture whose height

has enabled it to inflict arguably the most extensive damage on London's urban character of any building in recent years.

The architectural problem with the Walkie Talkie began life as a commercial solution. Commercial tenants are prepared to pay more money for higher views but accepted wisdom maintains that if tall buildings are going to be integrated into historic areas, they usually taper or get smaller as they reach the top in order to minimise their impact on the surrounding cityscape. This tenuous truce is evident in many of London's recent tranche of tall buildings including the Leadenhall Building, St Mary Axe (the 'Gherkin'), 52 Lime Street (the 'Scalpel') and, most notably, the Shard. A tapering envelope, however, means smaller floors at the top of the building where commercial tenants are prepared to pay most for those panoramic views, so the Walkie Talkie quite literally turns convention on its head by making the building get wider as it goes upwards. Commercially, it is a masterstroke as it means that the best views and thereby the most expensive tenancies, can be accrued on the largest floorplates. But from the perspective of London's urban character, the effect has been absolutely devastating.

The Walkie Talkie sits amongst a wizened labyrinth of narrow medieval streets and alleyways, all of which are now utterly overshadowed by its swollen, tumescent form. Its bulbous, domineering silhouette rises incongruously from its historic streetscape, wreaking visual havoc on the meandering and intricately composed urban character of nearby routes such as Lombard Street and Lovat Lane (Fig.91).

There is a mistaken belief that what matters most with tall buildings is how they meet the ground but here too the Walkie Talkie fails spectacularly. Instead of engaging with the lively streetscape that surrounds its base, it slams into Fenchurch Street and offers nothing to its immediate environs other than a squat, sterile lobby surmounted by a boorish bandana of ventilation louvres. In skyline terms too, the tower fails abysmally. In as much as the City has a skyline policy, it states that tall buildings should be concentrated in what is rather optimistically

91 20 Fenchurch Street, otherwise known as the 'Walkie Talkie', looms apocalyptically over Lombard Street.

termed the 'Eastern Cluster'. But the Walkie Talkie is located significantly south of the cluster, affording the tower a spatial isolation and visual prominence that not only renders its architectural defects more painfully apparent but also inflicts further disruption to an already disjointed urban skyline.

The cluster issue goes to the heart of why the Walkie Talkie was built in the first place and what we can do to avoid similar mistakes in the future. For, at its core, the building is as much a planning error as it is an architectural one. Despite its cluster dislocation forming a serious contravention of City planning policy, the building was still awarded planning permission. Moreover, it was even supported by the government's former design body CABE (the Commission for Architecture and the Built Environment), who once described the skyscraper as 'a successful scheme that would enhance the experience of a world city'.[26] An unusual confluence of circumstances allowed this to happen. The Corporation of London was determined to expand the office capacity of the city, City Hall was led by a mayor who was ideologically minded to support tall buildings and one can only assume that CABE, bedazzled by the involvement of a world-renowned so-called 'starchitect', was blinded to the serious design deficiencies the building contained.

Yes, the Walkie Talkie offers generous and free public access to its rooftop sky garden, which contains a public bar and restaurant and from which spectacular views can be seen. But this fails to override the fact that, yet again, the building savagely demonstrates what harm can be caused to London's character by the absence of a coherent and definitive city-wide tall buildings policy framework that is explicit in stating where tall buildings are and are not appropriate, sets clear contextual parameters to which the design of tall buildings must adhere, promotes genuine high-quality architecture and encapsulates a clear vision for what the city is and how tall buildings can be incorporated without undue harm to its all-important historic fabric and urban character. Without it, all London's urban character is going to get is more and more of the Walkie Talkie's corrosive legacy, namely that of an incongruous glass gargoyle graffitied onto the skyline of London (Fig.92).

92   In terms of height, form, materiality and townscape, 20 Fenchurch Street has a devastating impact on its local historic character.

## 22 BISHOPSGATE, CITY OF LONDON

- ✦ **Architect:** PLP
- ✦ **Client:** Lipton Rogers Developments
- ✦ **Type:** Office
- ✦ **Completion:** 2020
- ✦ **Harm:** Alleyways, Climate, Entrances, Height, Planning, Streets, Views

Standing 278 m (912 ft) high and with 62 storeys, 22 Bishopsgate is currently the tallest building in the City and the second tallest in the UK after the Shard. It is also quite possibly the most damaging building ever built in the City of London. Imagine the multiple failings of the nearby Walkie Talkie amplified onto a building more than twice its size.

Its first and most obvious mode of destruction is its scale. Although the tallest building in the City, 22 Bishopsgate is 32 m (105 ft) and several storeys shorter than the Shard. Equally, London is of course eminently comfortable with big buildings; the Shard is the tallest building in western Europe, Buckingham Palace is the largest functioning palace in northern Europe and St Paul's has the second largest classical dome in the world. But the gigantic, unleavened bulk of 22 Bishopsgate sets new standards for contextual impropriety. With 130,000 sq m (1.4 million sq ft) of area it offers more space than the Walkie Talkie and the nearby Leadenhall Building (the 'Cheesegrater') combined and provides roughly the same amount of additional floor space the entire city of Birmingham has aspired to provide over the next 20 years.[27] Additionally, at 80 m (262 ft) wide it is almost three times as wide as the M25. This might have been acceptable in the middle of established high-rise centres in denser and more modern cities like Shanghai, New York or Toronto. But incredibly this is been allowed to happen in London's oldest and most historic district, in an area noted for centuries

for its fine grain and narrow plots. The tower severs these intricate patterns and condemns virtually everything around it, office skyscrapers and historic buildings alike, to the diminished status of a Lilliputian toy (Fig.93).

Now, both London and the City need big office buildings to sustain its position as the world's financial centre. And this scale might well have been more successfully accommodated within an exceptional piece of architecture. But, alas, this is not the case. 22 Bishopsgate essentially presents itself as a relentless slab of glass and steel, an anodyne shaft which hurtles up to its full height with absolutely no attempt at the tapering, articulation or softening of summit that might be construed to mitigate the impact of its obscene bulk in a historic area. Instead we get a hazy, lazy horizontal stack of floor after floor piled pitilessly on top of each other with a series of weak, staggered offsets on the floorplate plan failing abysmally in their attempts to introduce the vertical segmentation that would help break down the building's overall mass. Given its size, it also hurls itself into an infinite number of views across

93   At 80m wide, 22 Bishopsgate is almost three times as wide as the M25 motorway.

94   In both width and height, 22 Bishopsgate completely overshadows Tower 42, once the UK's tallest building.

London, an aggressively mediocre incursion onto familiar townscape panoramas (Fig.94).

How did London come to this? Blame lies with the familiar tyrannical triumvirate of money, design and planning. The site was acquired in 2015 for an astonishing £300 million, a vastly inflated sum which has naturally compelled the owners to squeeze as much floor space onto it as physically possible in an effort to make a return on their investment. Next comes a fraught design history. The tower replaces an earlier design commonly known as the Pinnacle and created by the same architects. First mooted in 2006 it did not fare much better than the current incarnation in design terms and was a resounding advocate of the 'Dubai perfume bottle' school of skyscraper form, duly and pithily christened the 'Helter Skelter' for its lamentable efforts. But at least, unlike the current building, it tapered towards a single summit point, even if it did so in the most complicated and

lugubrious way possible. Only the seven-storey stump of its concrete core was ever built as the economic crash at the end of the last decade mercifully consigned the plans to history. The current, redesigned building therefore forms its simpler and cheaper replacement.

But once more the biggest culprit is London's planning system. Yet again the capital suffers because of the abject refusal of its planning hierarchy to institute a coherent, city-wide tall buildings policy framework that determines where tall buildings should and should not be built, forensically quantifies their impact and demands that they adhere to the very highest standards of architectural design. 22 Bishopsgate is the result of this vacuum and embodies the absolute triumph of the City's presumed commercial requirements over every other townscape, heritage, character or skyline concern. It thereby destroys the world-renowned historic and architectural reputation of the City of London and effectively helps turn the City's already chaotic skyline into an urban cabinet of yet more glass-fronted architectural grotesques. Yes, 22 Bishopsgate incorporates a whole host of genuine state-of-the-art technological innovations such as a biometric face recognition security system and a facade inspired by the aerodynamic principles of Formula One. But these will be outdated in just 10 years' time, while the harm the building has inflicted will still be as fresh as on the day it opened. How ironic that the tower's co-developer Stuart Lipton should once condemn 5 Broadgate for being 'the worst large building in the City for 20 years'[28] when he himself was to go on to help author a building that has wrecked the City's character and credibility for generations to come.

## CHAPTER SPITALFIELDS, TOWER HAMLETS

- ✦ **Architect:** TP Bennett
- ✦ **Client:** Nido Student Living
- ✦ **Type:** Residential
- ✦ **Completion:** 2010
- ✦ **Harm:** Alleyways, Climate, Colour, Grain, Height, Housing, Materials, Planning, Streets, Style, Views

With few notable exceptions, such as Maccreanor Lavington's One Cartwright Gardens and Henley Halebrown's exquisite Chadwick Hall in Roehampton, London student housing is generally of disappointing architectural quality, a trend sadly replicated across the UK. But arguably one of the worst examples is Chapter Spitalfields. The introduction of student tuition fees by the Labour government in 1998 may have established a totemic wave of student grievance whose political impact is still being felt today, but it also enabled millions of pounds to flood into the higher education sector. Much of this was spent on new student housing, usually built for, rather than by, universities, and by 2006 this sector had become so lucrative that it compelled the developer team who already had planning permission for a 25-storey office block in London's East End to submit a revised planning application for a 34-storey student housing tower. The result is the 112 m (367 ft) tall Chapter, previously the Nido Spitalfields block, which desecrates the skyline and townscape of the historic district from which takes its name.

For some time now, Spitalfields has been an unwitting battleground between heritage and redevelopment. Though it contains a stellar assortment of historic alleyways, famous markets and fine, early Georgian streets and terraces, its strategic position, sandwiched between the City of London and the less affluent East End, has meant that over the past 30 years it has consistently come under redevelopment pressure from the City's inevitable commercial expansion eastwards. In the 1990s, local and heritage campaigners lost a fierce battle with developers controversially planning to demolish at least half of the historic Spitalfields Market and the result is the anodyne Foster + Partners office block we see there today. The proposed redevelopment of the adjacent Bishopsgate Goodsyard which threatened to overshadow Spitalfields with a wall of skyscrapers has been another totemic conservation vs redevelopment flashpoint over the past decade. Perhaps as a result of these touchstone distractions, Chapter Spitalfields was able to slip quietly through the net (Fig.95).

95   Chapter Spitalfields is totally out of keeping with the scale and grain of its surrounding historic fabric.

And more is the pity. In a neighbourhood that, for the time being at least, remains historically low-rise, Chapter Spitalfields rises like a brutal, incongruous and insensitive sore thumb standing in ludicrous physical and typological isolation from the scale, grain and character of its local urban fabric. Were its completely inappropriate height the only issue, this would be bad enough. But the building piles insult upon injury by assuming a squat, slab-like rectilinear form which, in a Faustian floorplate pact, is only able to retain its slender side profiles by having distended front and back elevations that quite literally crash into views from all directions like a door slammed furiously into an invisible wall. And to top it all, the tower's facades, a pixelated, abstracted miasma of anodised barcode cladding popular in the 2000s but already laughably out of date, adds further visual discordancy and fragmentation to their already besieged local surroundings. In any neighbourhood, this level of architectural insensitivity would have been devastating. But in an area comprising a dense, historic patchwork of winding alleyways, Chapter Spitalfields causes irreparable harm to the coherence and rhythm of local townscape and seriously undermines the impact and integrity of both local and wider urban character.

## ME LONDON HOTEL, ALDWYCH/ CITY OF WESTMINSTER

+ **Architect:** Foster + Partners
+ **Client:** Various
+ **Type:** Melia Hotels International
+ **Completion:** 2013
+ **Harm:** Entrances, Materials, Streets, Topography, Views

The ME London Hotel does not so much harm London's character as squander a fantastic opportunity to enhance or at least reinforce it. The great imperial crescent of Aldwych is one of London's most grandiose formal urban set-pieces. While Aldwych sports a virtually continuous sweep of magnificent Edwardian neo-baroque frontages, the geometry of its curvature is calibrated by

96 The ME London Hotel marks a weak and feeble culmination to a series of critical urban set-pieces.

three main anchor buildings to the east, middle (north) and west of the crescent that all terminate vistas that radiate out in these three different directions. To the east, there is Australia House, a mighty rusticated heap of arches, statuary and colonnades that arguably forms London's finest purpose-built diplomatic mission. To the north sits Bush House, its monumental screened niche marking the centre point of the northern 'bow' of the crescent and forming a dramatic axial focus for the straight vista that extends along Kingsway. And facing down the Strand sits the new ME Hotel, the first hotel to be designed in its entirety by the world-famous architectural practice Foster + Partners (Fig.96).

In many ways the new hotel makes great efforts to be contextually sensitive. Like practically all of Aldwych it is faced in Portland stone. Also in keeping with standard Aldwych Edwardiana, it is solid and bulky and topped with a dark Mansard roof. The project also incorporates the welcome restoration of the ornate Marconi House next door and contains some stunning interiors, many of which are a moody, stylised and abstracted London version of boutique Las Vegas baroque. The problems as far as London's character go, begin with the limp and vapid articulation of the facades.

97  Regardless of stylistic differences, No. 1 City Road by William Lewis (1929) shows the massing, articulation and composition required to convincingly turn a corner.

Elevationally, the windows are formed by narrow oriel slits cut into the walls which lend the building an overly defensive, fortress-like demeanour whose deadpan dullness is utterly at odds with the festive gaiety of its surrounding buildings. The effect may well be polite, but it is also pedestrian, an abject lesson in the perils of compartmentalising character and context into nothing more than a mechanistic adherence to building heights and materials.

But worse is to come at the pivotal corner that forms the western tip of the Aldwych crescent. Turning a corner well is an essential cosmopolitan

requirement for London buildings, as corners offer multiple architectural opportunities to proudly celebrate the angular awkwardness of the capital's irregular layout. They also potentially allow moments of kinetic townscape drama in a city whose haphazard sprawl instinctively suppresses the formal architectural set-piece. And finally, in a traditionally low-rise city, they also present relatively rare opportunities for strident vertical expression. Accordingly London offers some fine precedents for turning corners. Nos. 1 Cornhill and City Road (Fig.97) do so with the reliably dynamic baroque device of a dome, and the recently refurbished No. 1 New Oxford Street channels its corner status through swish and decadent art deco curves. Even the famous corner of Sir James Stirling's controversial No. 1 Poultry piles one three-dimensional shape on top of another to form a stacked, multicoloured prow that has all the balletic thrust of a ship's proudly projecting figurehead.

Not so here at Aldwych. A thin, emaciated cylinder forms the corner climax, lazily inscribed with the same oriel strips we have witnessed on the side facades. Attempts to add additional gravitas are equally ineffectual. Vertical grooves cut into the cylinder merely render it weaker and more skeletal and a preposterous glass attic lantern provides a scrawny centrepiece to the entire ensemble and bears all the compositional conviction of a hastily donned toupee. All this at a location whose kinetic hinge status could have forged an architecture that dramatically expressed rather than suppressed the great townscape pivot on which this landmark crescent corner sits. Ironically, a building that did just that was Bassett and Keeling's great Gaiety Theatre that stood on this very same site from 1903 until its tragic demolition in 1956. Decked out with mighty colonnades and dripping with statuary, this was a riotous piece of Edwardian baroque more stylistically and contextually attuned to the rest of Aldwych. But its success was not so much a question of style as composition, as its deep attic loggias and high-mounted corner dome skilfully and powerfully negotiated the various axes and forces that pivoted through and around the site. In so doing, the old theatre flamboyantly affirmed its dynamic role within the Aldwych set-piece and theatrically enshrined London's tradition of corner celebrations. The ME Hotel may not actively harm its surroundings, but if the contribution its Edwardian predecessor made to London's character can be categorised as a bang, then its own must be disregarded as a whimper.

## NINE ELMS, BATTERSEA/LONDON BOROUGH OF WANDSWORTH

✦ **Architect:** Various
✦ **Client:** Various
✦ **Type:** Mixed use
✦ **Completion:** Ongoing
✦ **Harm:** Density, Height, Housing, Planning, Squares, Streets, Transport, Uses, Views, Waterways

If King's Cross Central is a stellar example of successful urban regeneration and a coherent masterplan then Nine Elms in south-west London is the polar opposite. Nine Elms is a massive £15 billion urban regeneration project that is currently London's biggest building site and is one of the largest regeneration projects of its kind in Europe. It aims to revitalise 227 hectares (561 acres) of riverside land between Battersea Power Station and Vauxhall Cross that was formerly largely underdeveloped, deindustrialised and derelict wasteland. The ambitious project aims to replace this with 20,000 homes, 25,000 permanent jobs, scores of new shops, restaurants and offices and even a new tube station on the extended London Underground Northern line. By far the biggest component is the conversion of the iconic Battersea Power Station into an £8 billion residential, office and leisure complex boasting 4,000 homes within and around the building's retained structural shell. While the overall project is not due for completion until the mid- to late 2020s, much has already been finished. This includes a number of residential towers, the partial realisation of the redevelopment masterplan for Battersea Power Station and the showpiece relocation of the US Embassy from its historic home in Georgian Mayfair into a new £1 billion super-embassy that in many ways has acted as the catalyst for the area's wider regeneration.

So, Nine Elms certainly does not lack ambition, but it is the poverty of its design, execution and social consciousness that has already caused such harm to London's character. One of the biggest problems with Nine Elms is the masterplan itself. Drawn up by the Nine Elms Partnership which comprises an impressive list of stakeholders including two local authorities and a number of developers, it is flabby and incoherent, lacking the tightness and definition evident at King's Cross and necessary for it to assume the vital role of constant conceptual anchor for a large and disparate scheme. Vacuous masterplans inevitably create vacuums, and into that vacuum all manner of urban toxicity has crept, further threatening urban character. A large part of the corrosion is due to a generally poor quality of design. A handful of new buildings do aspire towards some kind of architectural integrity, Allies and Morrison's elegant and experimental 35-storey brick tower at Keybridge House, the UK's tallest brick-clad structure, is one such rare example. But the majority of its buildings are characterised by the kind of anodyne, anonymous sterility which reduces architecture to a masonry costume husk protecting the developer-led floorplates in whose maximisation commercial priority has been solely invested. The conversion of Battersea Power Station itself typifies this trend and the famed structure is set to endure indefinite humiliation by being surrounded by a girdle of towering curved-glass crescent blocks clearly conceived to maximise the returns that will help indemnify the massive cost of restoring the power station in the first place.

The issue of maximisation leads to another caustic inevitability at Nine Elms: the stifling preponderance of tall buildings. The rampant opportunism unleashed by the loose masterplan and the strategic relegation of design has left the door wide open to the proliferation of tall buildings and the flagrant commercial profiteering they can engender. The fact that there is no historic precedent whatsoever for tall buildings in this district has not stopped scores of towers being built and proposed, some of which are up to 60 storeys high, taller than anything that currently exists at Canary Wharf. In fact, so ruthless is this propensity that one of the few notable works of contemporary architecture in the area, Arup's futuristic ski-slope

98　Nine Elms appears as an incoherent and uncoordinated glut of autonomously conceived high-rise buildings.

bus station at Vauxhall, only built in 2004, is already earmarked for demolition and replacement by skyscrapers.

These and Nine Elms' other tranche of towers promise not only to drastically and irresponsibly alter the character of this part of London but to grievously undermine that of adjacent neighbourhoods on whose townscape these mammoth structures will inevitably intrude (Fig.98). The steroidal syringe that is Broadway Malyan's St George Wharf Tower was the first to set the trend, barging its mediocre way into unwarranted prominence beside views of Parliament's Victoria Tower at Westminster. But it has now been joined by a host of equally inane successors, many of which are typified by the discordance of Rolfe Judd's Nine Elms Point, a building of such angular awkwardness that it appears to be a number of

different shapes and cladding systems furiously flung together in the dark. The fact that it offers absolutely no contextual engagement and seems to have been designed in complete isolation from its neighbouring towers is sadly symptomatic of the entire Nine Elms development.

But arguably the saddest and most damaging aspect of Nine Elms is the insidious social exclusivity it is enforcing. The vast majority of its towers offer luxury residential accommodation that is often used as an investment bolthole for foreign buyers. London has been awash with international money for centuries and it is a key ingredient in the city's globalist, mercantile outlook and heritage. But the coveting and concentration of this type of investment at Nine Elms, coupled with the paltry provision of affordable housing, threatens to turn the district into an uninhabited luxury ghetto without the social fabric or community on which urban character and true regeneration fundamentally rely.

## NOVA VICTORIA, VICTORIA/CITY OF WESTMINSTER

+ **Architect:** PLP, Benson & Forsyth
+ **Client:** Land Securities
+ **Type:** Office/Residential/Leisure
+ **Completion:** 2016
+ **Harm:** Colour, Grain, Height, Planning, Streets, Views

Victoria Street has always had an awkward presence on the London urban scene. When it was laid out as a slum-clearance scheme in 1851, it was lined with what were then considered tall, red-brick residential blocks that incorporated shops on their ground floors. While these buildings would invariably be listed today, by the 1940s London had grown weary with what was perceived as dour Victoriana and it was with minimal architectural regret that the street was virtually flattened by the Blitz in the Second World War.

Then followed a programme of extensive redevelopment in the 1960s and 1970s where the shops remained but the flats were replaced with waves of inhuman podium slab office blocks above, effectively replacing one form of urban devastation with another. Since the 2000s many of these buildings have been redeveloped, with only moderately less harmful results. But by far the most grievous offender is Nova Victoria, which sits on its western end and is one of the worst office developments central London has ever seen (Fig.99).

To understand why one must first understand the character of Victoria and its surrounding areas. Since the war, Victoria has evolved into a somewhat discordant mix of Victorian hotels and terraced frontages nestling around a series of unsympathetic post-war buildings, the chief offender of which was previously Howard Fairbairn & Partners' Portland House, 32 storeys of bleak brutalist menace at the centre of an impenetrable (but obligatory) 1960s gyratory. Wrecking views from the nearby Buckingham Palace Rond Point, Portland House set

99   With its garish colours, crude geometry and inappropriate scale, Nova Victoria represents one of central London's gravest planning mistakes outside the City in recent years.

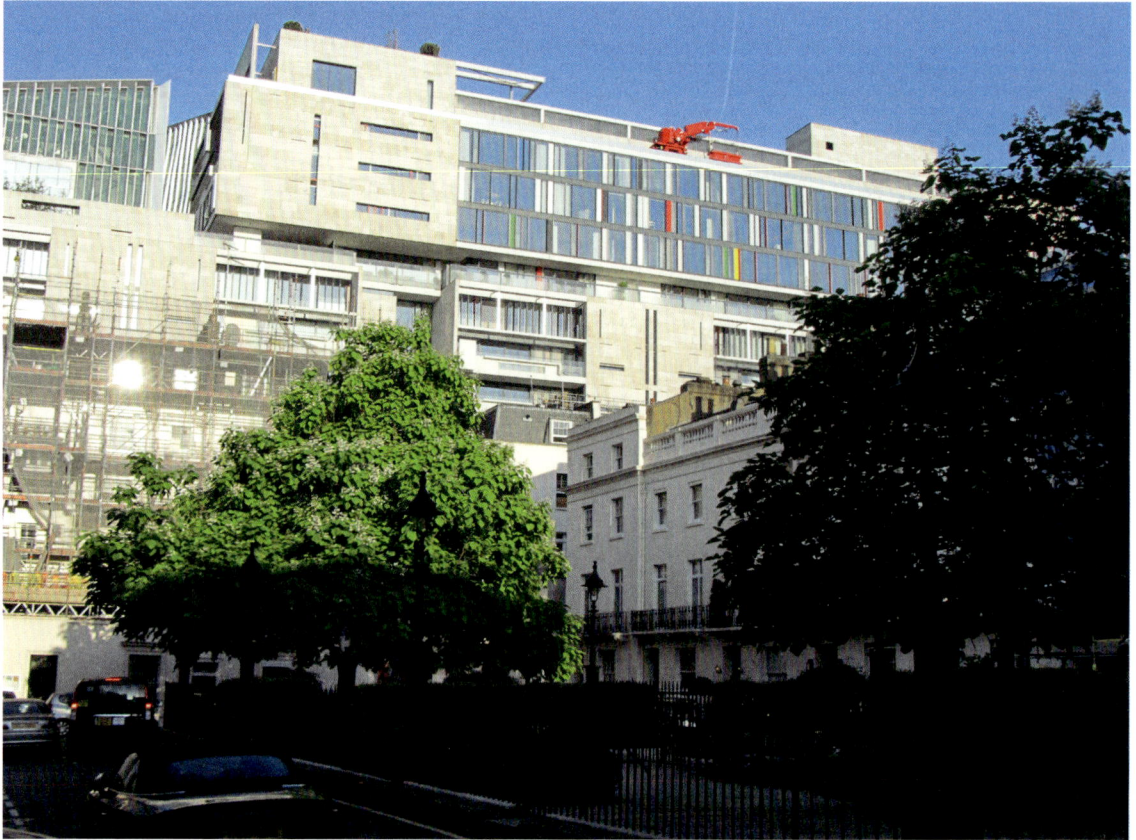

100    The view from nearby Victoria Square reveals the catastrophic impact Nova Victoria has on its local historic context.

a precedent of reckless incongruity that invariably gave impunity to future violations such as Nova Victoria itself. It also gave licence to ignore the superb heritage assets located just a stone's throw away from Victoria, such as the palatial 19th-century stucco terraces of Pimlico and Belgravia, and Buckingham Palace itself.

This is a licence that has been enthusiastically utilised by Nova. The scheme comprises five main blocks and in its first phase two are offices and the third is residential. The residential block by Benson & Forsyth is the first cause for concern. At very nearly twice the height of adjacent stucco and red-brick terraces and comprising an abstract facade of incoherent extrusions and random sliced openings, it is slammed onto Buckingham Palace Road. The

sheer scale of contextual harm it unleashes is evident from adjacent Victoria Square, where it looms over elegant stucco townhouses (Fig.100).

Even worse is the pair of glass office blocks behind. A horrific pair of sliced and chamfered towers stagger awkwardly up to their full height of 18 storeys, thus ensuring they join Portland House in its ruination of the backdrop to Buckingham Palace. Each tower is clad in a relentless, unleavened sheath of asymmetrically swirling fins that gather around triangular openings at their base and whose jagged profiles appear to make the buildings look as if they are in an advanced state of disintegration. To make matters worse, an assortment of bright red prows are smeared across various points of the exterior like war paint (Fig.101).

101  Nova Victoria's unwarranted intrusion onto the iconic and internationally significant view of Buckingham Palace shows the casual irresponsibility with which London's historic character is increasingly being compromised.

The impact these new buildings have on local character is devastating. If we picture the urban fabric of Victoria, Pimlico and Belgravia as an intricate patchwork of linear terraces stitched onto a needlepoint underlay of squares, streets and parks and imagine a knife slicing through this delicate embroidery, the Nova Victoria development amounts to trying to fix the damage with lead. It is, sadly, symptomatic of several new developments which are eroding London's character. First comes the incremental accumulation of smaller buildings consistent with local grain into a bigger site more convenient for single development but at odds with surrounding scale. Then follows the regeneration ransom of urban 'improvements' being sought at any cost and certainly at the expense of appropriate or high-quality architecture. Grossly over-scaled and laboriously overdeveloped, Nova Victoria sets a new benchmark for dystopian dysfunction that is completely at odds with local character and context.

# ONE NEW CHANGE, CITY OF LONDON

✦ **Architect:** Jean Nouvel
✦ **Client:** Land Securities
✦ **Type:** Office/Retail/Leisure
✦ **Completion:** 2010
✦ **Harm:** Colour, Materials, Planning, Streets, Style, Views

The tragic irony about One New Change is that it actually does three things very well indeed. Firstly, its 60 shops (which form the City's only shopping centre) reintroduce retail into a part of London overwhelmingly associated with a financial, corporate monoculture and thereby mark a brave, transformative attempt to elongate the social fabric of the City into evenings and weekends. Appropriately, before the modern onslaught of banks and offices, Cheapside on which One New Change is located was effectively the City's principal medieval high street.

Secondly, One New Change re-establishes ancient, bygone pedestrian routes in the City of London that had previously disappeared after centuries of redevelopment. The passageways created by its cruciform plan echo these historic connections and seamlessly embed the development into the historic pattern, fabric and grain of the City and, in particular, open up a brand-new vista from which to appreciate the eastern facade of St Paul's Cathedral. With One New Change's zig-zagging asymmetrical glass facades impaling a distorted tripartite reflection of the cathedral onto the climax of this vista, we get a stirringly dynamic architectural representation of Anthony van Dyck's iconic *Triple Portrait of Charles I*. Thirdly, and most importantly, in its sumptuous new rooftop terrace piazza – one of the largest of its kind in Europe – the development opens up yet more previously unseen views of the cathedral and also delivers a virtuoso and blisteringly innovative adaptation of conventional London public space assembly and supply.

To varying degrees, all these elements enhance London's urban character. But, alas, they are outweighed by the huge damage inflicted on

102　With its muddy pallor and amorphous shape, One New Change is a belligerently mediocre neighbour to St Paul's.

that same character by the shape, materiality and townscape impact of the development. The architect, Jean Nouvel, describes his building as the 'stealth bomber',[29] a reference to the low-slung composition it was forced to assume in order to circumnavigate protected views of St Paul's. But what One New Change lacks in height, it makes up for in hostility, for the building refuses to harmonise with its surrounding historic context. Its amorphous form of folded planes and swerving angles is the most obvious aggressor, peeping provocatively into the historic view of the cathedral from Watling Street and ensuring that the rectilinear townscape rhythms established by neighbouring buildings are comprehensively undermined (Fig.102).

The glass in which the building is encased also feels alien and anodyne against the heavier brick and stone that surrounds it. And the murky brown tones in which the building's external envelope are covered, with sacrificial dashes of Nouvel trademark red, exude a dingy pallor. Of course, the kind of contrast which One New Change represents is an intrinsic part of London's character too. But it has a time and a place, and engaging in such a nihilistic and narcissistic version of it here, at the precise location where London's fabric is meant to defer to St Paul's rather than demand attention of its own, marks a selfish and needlessly aggressive destabilisation of the nature of background townscape character and composition.

# Projects that Enhance London's Urban Character

- ✦ 60 Queen Victoria Street
- ✦ Chichester Rents
- ✦ Eccleston Yards
- ✦ King's Cross Central
- ✦ McGrath Road
- ✦ Newport Street Gallery
- ✦ One Cartwright Gardens
- ✦ The Shard

## 60 QUEEN VICTORIA STREET, CITY OF LONDON

- ✦ **Architect:** Foggo Associates
- ✦ **Client:** Heron Property Corporation
- ✦ **Type:** Office
- ✦ **Completion:** 2000
- ✦ **Benefit:** Colour, Grain, Height, Materials, Style

How do you reference context without copying it? It is a simple question and one particularly pertinent to the fundamental problem of how you enhance historic urban character without creating legions of buildings that all subscribe to the same pseudo-historicist pastiche. It is also a question uniquely pertinent to the City of London, London's oldest district. The City offers scores of office blocks which choose to ignore their context and benefit from a planning system that either tacitly or actively allows them to. The globalist proliferation of tall buildings in the City, most of which are bland steel and glass boxes that say nothing of the character or heritage of their surroundings, is the most caustic and conspicuous example of this trend. But there is also a tradition of modern office blocks that have tried to forge a brand of contemporary architecture that seeks to engage and empathise with the rich historic fabric that surrounds them. Minster Court, GMW Architects' maniacally peculiar neo-Gothic citadel, attempts to do this with cartoonish superficiality. Moulded from the same postmodernist stable is Sir James Stirling's landmark No. 1 Poultry which appropriates a whole slew of classical references in a more scholarly and mature way. And across the street, Norman Foster's recent Bloomberg Building is deliberately dressed in exactly the same Derbyshire sandstone as John Whichcord Jr's exquisite City of London Magistrates Court of 1873.

103   With its defensive bronze exterior 60 Queen Victoria Street forms a high-tech version of a medieval keep.

One of the City's most intriguing and convincing examples of the contemporary historic reference office blocks, however, is sandwiched between No. 1 Poultry and Bloomberg and enjoys a significantly lower profile than either of them. 60 Queen Victoria Street occupies a triangular block and, relatively unusually for the City these days, is only nine storeys high. Peter Foggo was an exponent of a softer, less abrasive high-tech aesthetic than his contemporaries Richard Rogers and Nicholas Grimshaw, and he brings this more measured functionalism to a number of other City office blocks. But of all of them, 60 Queen Victoria Street makes the most potent contribution to London's character by effectively adopting a whimsical high-tech hybrid that transforms the building into a vigorous contemporary rendition of a barricaded Gothic fortress or an armour-plated medieval keep. The building immediately demands attention by being clad in bronze panels, an uncommon fascia in the City. But with its vividly stained and weathered patina, the block instantly appears to have stood in rusty defiance for 100 years. Rather than the faceless elevational anonymity so often applied to modern City office blocks, each window here is individually defined within a bay and then shielded behind a heavy tripartite *brise soleil* that appears like an intricately woven plate of armour. Snaking up the facade are slender paired rods that appear like vertical, orthogonal representations of the delicate lierne vaulting over a cathedral nave. Here too the rods cluster down onto thicker piers at their base and are supported by delicately cantilevering brackets that form a shallow colonnade and seem like the wistfully retained halves of a slender bronze aisle of missing pointed arches (Fig.103).

In its mechanistic structural expressionism, 60 Queen Victoria Street provides a vivid reanimation of Gothic architecture, studiously exposing the multiple interesting and unexpected parallels it shares with the high-tech style. And in so doing it forcefully aligns itself with the medieval heritage of the City, cleverly deploying a contemporary palette of colour, materials and extruded elevational articulation to enhance historic character. This character is further enhanced by the building's provision of modern office space within a mid-rise format more in

104 The extruded steel exoskeleton arcade that runs along the ground floor is reminiscent of the ribs of broken Gothic arches.

105 With its emphasis on verticality and fortification, 60 Queen Victoria Street relates directly the City's Gothic heritage and character.

keeping with the City's historic townscape than the high-rise either consciously or unconsciously primed to unsettle it. And in its narrow vertical bay articulation, the building adheres to the City's more intricate streetscape grain. While Gothic features extensively on the City's churches it is less evident in its commercial architecture and 60 Queen Victoria Street provides one of the most stirring adaptations of the style to the streetscape office template since R.L. Roumieu's fantastic 33–5 Eastcheap of 1868 (Figs 104 and 105).

The streetscape perspective is important too. For all its dynamic articulation, 60 Queen Victoria Street is a work of carefully stitched background architecture. Unlike many of its more egotistical contemporary equivalents, it dissolves humbly into the streetscape but is no less important due to the fact that it helps provide the vivid and essential urban backdrop onto which urban character can be etched. There are inevitably flaws to the project. Its shallow ground-floor arcade exudes awkward spatial redundancy and its rooftop *brise soleil* forms a flat and anticlimactic horizontal lid where a more kinetically mechanised crescendo in the charged spirit of the lower facade might have been more exhilarating. But were more City office buildings to attempt to bridge the gap between the City's past and present with as much enigmatic virtuosity as this, then the City's character would be afforded far better protection than is currently the case.

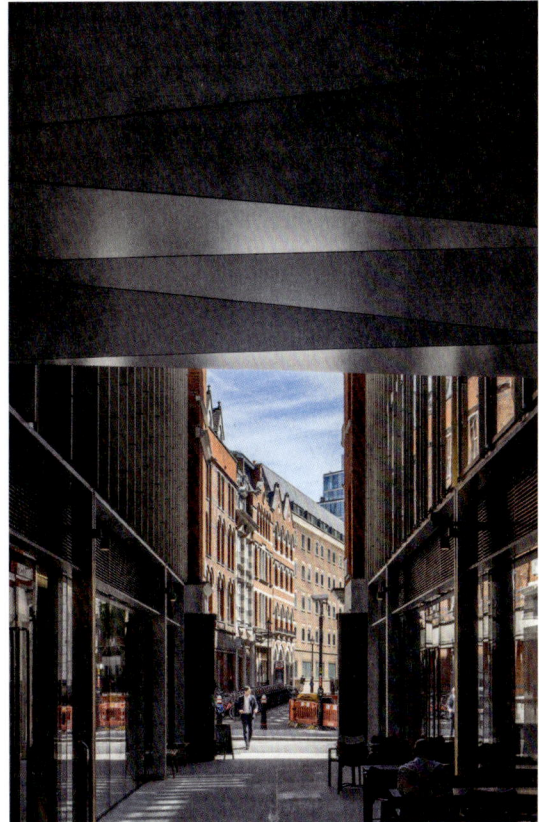

106  Chichester Rents: the rejuvenated alleyway retains its integration into the surrounding street grid.

# CHICHESTER RENTS, CAMDEN/ CITY OF LONDON

+ **Architect:** ORMS
+ **Client:** Raingate Limited
+ **Type:** Office/Public Realm
+ **Completion:** 2017
+ **Benefit:** Alleyways, Entrances, Grid, Lighting, Materials, Names, Style, Views

Chichester Rents is one of those quizzically endearing historic street names that are a unique and quirky part of London's character. The title refers to City of London lands once owned by the Bishops of Chichester and the rents levied on their tenants therein. Today, Chichester Rents refers to a Victorian commercial building built on one of the bishops' lands on Chancery Lane, the narrow thoroughfare that is essentially the bustling high street in London's legal district. Even narrower is the historic City alleyway that cuts Chichester Rents in half and is part of an extraordinary network of tiny hidden alleyways, lanes and courtyards that straddle the City in general, but is particularly prevalent in the area around Fleet Street and the various historic Inns of Court. Prior to 2017, Chichester Rents was a fairly unremarkable and unprepossessing pedestrian link spanned by two postmodern, lightweight, multilevel bridge structures at either end. But the opportunity arose

107  Chichester Rents uses splayed geometries and metallic materials to form a dynamic abstraction of traditional City alleyway characteristics.

108  By effecting sinking the alleyway beneath an expanded chamfered bridge, Chichester Rents accentuates the sense of concealment and surprise that are common characteristics of City alleys.

to refurbish the two Victorian wings on either side and revitalise the alleyway that divided them. The result provides a rare opportunity to construct a contemporary reinterpretation of a historic City alleyway and reaffirm enormous urban and spatial value to the character of London and the City itself (Fig.106).

Gone are the two dour pedestrian bridges. In their place an extraordinary stepped infill structure has been installed that straddles the full length of the alleyway at the top floor but – at both front and back – successively recedes on every level below until it forms a roof for the passageway at its shortest point. Cleverly, this solution increases the

amount of internal floor area the bridge provides in comparison to the previous twin narrow bridge format, doubtless generating additional rental income to help justify the cost of refurbishment. But its impact on the alleyway is far more melodramatic. Instantly, the alley is transformed from an open lane to a covered passageway whose resulting darker nature is perfectly in keeping with the more brooding, atmospheric character of other nearby alleys (Fig.107).

The infill structure itself is a work of energised kinetic choreography. Improbably, but decadently clad in shiny, anodised aluminium panels that enable the infill to resemble a jewel clasped between two clenched masonry fists, each stepped recess floor level is set at an alternating oblique angle to the one above and below. This forms a faceted three-dimensional concertina structure that hurtles and gyrates downwards like a series of weighty arrows pointing inevitably to the passageway below. When viewed from Chancery Lane, this stepped cluster of zany angles not only acts as a frenetic metaphor for the haphazard layout of London's historic alleyways, but also transforms the mouth of the alleyway into a gaping, angular portal that, in the tradition of all the best London alleyways, makes it virtually impossible not to succumb to intrigue and inspection. Best of all, by the development creating a new perpendicular link between Chichester Rents and the adjacent alleyway of Bishops Court, it wisely embeds itself into the grain and pattern of the surrounding historic routes and fabric (Fig.108).

Chichester Rents does have its flaws. Though largely encased within an anodyne 1980s steel and brickwork shell, the old alleyway offered a shabby but charming mix of long-established and well-patronised retail premises including a cafe, tailor and florist and came complete with quaint hanging shop signs. These have been replaced with a more upmarket assortment of gym, coffee shop and trendy street eatery. Therefore, while inevitably smarter, it feels colder and more corporate and is part of a disturbing pattern of mummified identikit chains homogenising the City's retail offering. Equally, the large square windows on each recessed level of the aluminium infill are probably too large and conspicuous to conform to the peeping discretion that alleyway etiquette normally requires. But these are perhaps small prices to pay for the raw revisionist thrill of witnessing the historic alleyway that forms such an immersive and atmospheric part of London's character dynamically and operatically reinvented for the 21st century.

## ECCLESTON YARDS, VICTORIA/ CITY OF WESTMINSTER

- ✦ **Architect:** BuckleyGrayYeoman
- ✦ **Client:** The Grosvenor Estate
- ✦ **Type:** Public Realm
- ✦ **Completion:** 2018

- ✦ **Benefit:** Alleyways, Art, Colour, Entrances, Furniture, Grain, Grid, Lighting, Materials, Names, Paving, Planning, Signage, Squares, Streets, Uses

In architecture, the term 'found space' popularly refers to awkward, leftover or forgotten spaces usually located within older buildings and discovered and repurposed for new uses during refurbishment or renovation works. In more colloquial terms, it can almost be described as accidental architecture. The same principle exists in urban design, and most cities contain series of forgotten spaces that are either intentionally or unintentionally revealed as a result of some kind of urban redevelopment venture and then adapted for brand-new uses. London, a city that revels in both the nook and the cranny, is crammed full of such spaces. At the larger end of the scale, the deindustrialised backlands of King's Cross Central can be described as a vast sequence of found spaces, as can Norman Foster's spectacular Great Court in the British Museum, which cleared away a cluttered knot of ancillary buildings in the centre of the museum to first reveal, and then reconstruct the dramatic courtyard space we see today. Equally, a pattern of inventively revitalised found spaces has developed in Covent Garden and its environs in recent years, and projects like Make Architects' St James's Market and, in particular, Kohn Pedersen Fox's Floral Court and Smith Caradoc-Hodgkins and MR Partnership's St Martin's Courtyard have all been marked by the radical exposure and reinterpretation of formerly hidden or ignored urban spaces.

One of the most interesting of these found space projects has been compiled on a much smaller and more modest scale, but the manner of its inspired transformation from forgotten, light industrial service yard to vibrant retail and restaurant hub, skilfully resonates with the special tones and nuances of London's character. Eccleston Yards lies on the boundary between Victoria and Belgravia in an area that, unlike the aforesaid Covent Garden examples, cannot rely on extremely high levels of pedestrian footfall and an already well-established retail and leisure economy as a virtual guarantor of commercial success. Prior to its 2018 overhaul, the area now known as Eccleston Yards was a forgotten service yard inelegantly overlooked by the backs of surrounding buildings. These buildings included an office, flats, small light industrial units and an electrical substation. The service yard itself, which was primarily used for parking, also contained a series of open brick shelters known as 'giraffe sheds', double-height, garage-like structures previously used by the electrical company for storage. Crucially, the courtyard was a dead end and while it was linked via a covered alleyway from the adjacent Eccleston Place, it offered no access to anywhere else.

In short, this forlorn car park was like thousands of forgotten backstreet hinterlands all over London. These spaces are easily dismissed but when ingeniously reinterpreted by the subtle and creative design strategies such as those employed at Eccleston Yards they reveal themselves as rich in the layered intricacies and soulful eccentricities that define London's character and are particularly evident in its clandestine, backstreet realms. Eccleston Yards has now been packaged as a creative enterprise hub and has been reborn as a slick, hard-landscaped public courtyard surrounded by trendy new commercial units containing bar, food, fashion, fitness and co-working outlets. Each of these units has been carefully inserted into the former rear facades that overlook the courtyard which means that, for the first time, the courtyard is faced by frontages rather than backs. The insertions have been handled with great sensitivity to the

existing fabric, some of which dates from the early 20th century (Fig.109).

To some extent, commercial redevelopments like this happen all the time in London, but what makes Eccleston Yards exceptional is the degree to which it harnesses the haphazard, discordant awkwardness of both of its former state and London's backstreet character in order to forge a vibrant new identity for its revitalised incarnation. Most evidently, the development's name eschews the more polished developer labels of 'courtyard' or 'square' and engages directly in a typology of rougher space that forms a key part of London's heritage and nostalgia. This is emphasised by the deliberately faded Eccleston Yards sign painted on two of its high-level walls. Additionally, the car park's irregular shape has been maintained and the central courtyard oozes into a whole series of mini-forecourts and awkward spatial pockets all around it, each one now cleverly and subtly re-utilised as a dedicated external vestibule for whatever new use has been allocated therein. The former giraffe sheds have been infilled with a glossy parade of chic glass-fronted restaurants. Also, the pedestrian link from Eccleston Place has been reimagined as a buoyant urban catwalk, with retained, rusty steel beams and an existing enclosed translucent bridge flying haphazardly overhead; one side is lined with a new sparkling skin of ceramic-glazed brickwork inspired by the Edwardian heritage of one of the courtyard's

109    Eccleston Yards form a vibrant reclamation of former concealed and utilitarian London backlands.

feature blocks. Glimpsing the courtyard through this narrow covered passageway from the Eccleston Place entrance also provides the voyeuristic urban thrill of peeping into normally hidden back gardens.

Throughout the development, a dynamic new lighting scheme illuminates some of the square's quirkier features, such as narrow recessed entrances and the aforesaid translucent bridge. Best of all, is a new link forged through to the adjacent Ebury Street, which means that for the first time Eccleston Yards becomes a route rather than a destination and is thereby overlaid onto London's intricate web of furrowed pedestrian shortcuts and connections. Emerging as if by surprise from a blind corner at the end of a narrow passageway from Ebury Street, the development also conforms to the tradition of oblique and staggered routes that London's organic grid imposes on its streetscape and the consequent spatial ritual of concealment, spontaneity and revelation this creates (Fig.110).

Doubtless all of this was easier to deliver because the landowner here is a single entity, the Grosvenor Estate. This kind of consistent ownership over various lands is a rare, serendipitous circumstance in much of the capital. But Eccleston Yards is a success not as a result of control, but of conception. For in its reinventive glorification of all the discarded detritus of the urban condition, ranging from metal escape stairs to garage huts, it forms a wistful ode to the messy, quirky, individualistic, irregular, colourful and whimsically odd otherworldliness of London's parallel backstreet world.

110   In true London fashion, Eccleston Place offers a relatively innocuous passageway entrance.

## KING'S CROSS CENTRAL, KING'S CROSS/LONDON BOROUGH OF CAMDEN

- ✦ **Architect:** Various, inc. Stanton Williams, Heatherwick Studio, Niall McLaughlin, WilkinsonEyre
- ✦ **Client:** Argent
- ✦ **Type:** Mixed-use
- ✦ **Completion:** Ongoing
- ✦ **Benefit:** Density, Fountains, Housing, Lighting, Planning, Squares, Style, Uses, Waterways

King's Cross was once the epitome of urban blight. Its eponymous station terminus was effectively strangled by a temporary concourse annexe that ended up remaining in place for almost 30 years. The magnificent St Pancras Station next door had only narrowly escaped demolition in the 1960s and had been trapped in a stasis of mismanaged decline ever since. The area around King's Cross itself frequently lapsed into a den of vice, vagrancy and criminality by night and sometimes by day. And the vast railway hinterlands behind the station, crippled by post-industrial dereliction, had long sunk into invisibility in the capital's public consciousness after having been colonised by a sporadically nefarious London backstreet mix of nightclubs, garages and gasholders.

Over the past 20 years, this forbidding dystopian concoction has been comprehensively transformed into one of the most dynamic and successful large-scale urban regeneration projects in London's recent history. This has been achieved by the development of an extraordinary masterplan that has not only effectively become the template for how to deliver mixed-use regeneration in the capital, but has also placed London's heritage and character at its spiritual core. The masterplan adopts a range of strategies to achieve this outcome and immerse itself into the rhythm and grain of London's character (Fig.111).

Perhaps the most obvious strategy is the skilful way in which new public space is woven into the development. In many ways, King's Cross Central can be perceived a series of public routes

141

111 King's Cross Central is a massive regeneration project that seeks to revitalise 54 hectares (133 acres) of formerly derelict industrial wasteland on both sides of the Regent's Canal.

separated by buildings, a brave reversal of the conventional floorplate-led approach that normally determines mixed-use development. The result is a sumptuous sequence of new public spaces that twists its way through the scheme and cleverly anchors it to its surrounding fabric in a way that immediately makes it feel like part of the city rather than a separate estate. King's Cross Square (site of the former concourse) by Stanton Williams and Granary Square by Townshend Landscape Architects are the largest, and both display a crisp refinement of layout, materials and surface treatment. The colourful choreographed fountain jets in Granary Square in particular add a vibrant theatricality and have become a firm favourite amongst locals and visitors. Interspersed around these principal spaces is a secondary network of new avenues, streets and squares whose diversity and informality instantly reference London's proud public space traditions.

Diversity is also used to reflect the wider character of London. Unlike standard commercial developments, King's Cross boasts an extraordinary mixture of uses to give it the feel and character of a neighbourhood in its own right. As well as the usual offices and the two railway

termini to its south, this also includes housing, a university, a school, shops, restaurants, gyms, community facilities, parks and hotels. Diversity also extends to the variety of architectural styles adopted, which ranges from contemporary to traditional and includes a host of traditional London building materials stretching from stone, brickwork and metal, to concrete, steel and glass. Essentially, in its sustained pursuit of multiplicity, King's Cross Central is a miniaturised version of the city that surrounds it.

Arguably, the most convincing way in which King's Cross embraces and enhances London's character is in its approach to heritage. King's Cross has always maintained a raw industrial atmosphere, far removed from the bourgeois gentility of Covent Garden or South Kensington. Railway sidings unfurl alongside train sheds and straddle a network of bridges and tunnels, all of which feed the two vast termini at the southern tip of the site. This is an area whose heritage has been forged by industry and infrastructure, and the masterplan is keen to reflect this. New buildings such as David Chipperfield's One Pancras Square sport moulded, cast-iron columns that recall the steely utilitarianism of Victorian railway architecture, and Stanton Williams's University of the Arts building features monumental shafts of exposed concrete which also reference the raw, blank muscularity of 19th-century industrial infrastructure. But it is in its sensitive and spirited adaptation of previously derelict historic buildings that King's Cross truly excels. The Granary Building, a monumental wheat warehouse of 1852, has been lovingly restored to become the mighty entrance block of Stanton Williams's aforesaid university. The site's most memorable and romantic features, a trio of disused gasholders, have been converted into flats by WilkinsonEyre, whose detailing and craftwork subtly recall the drive and energy of the industrial age in which their circular hosts were forged (Fig.112).

Most melodramatic of all is Coal Drops Yard, a pair of Victorian brick warehouses sumptuously reimagined by Heatherwick Studio. The two near-parallel warehouses have been restored and converted into retail premises with the space between them reconfigured as an open piazza. But the crowning glories are the slate roofs of

112   At Gasholders, WilkinsonEyre has ingeniously inserted new housing into the retained Victorian cylindrical structures that are revered remnants of the industrial past of King's Cross.

113   Heatherwick Studio's barnstorming conversion of parallel railway sidings at Coal Drops Yard challenges conservation convention by placing two bulging, expanded Victorian roofs over a new retail plaza.

each warehouse which, as they reach the centre of each opposing block, ripple and bulge out towards each other before touching at their centres above an exposed glass attic to form an improbable, yet endearing engineered, cantilever kiss. It is an astonishing gesture, bristling with enigmatic wit and sculptural energy and charged with an electrifying sense of operatic spectacle that blurs the boundaries between architecture and performance. It also forms an incredibly audacious treatise on how contemporary intervention can both sympathise with and stimulate heritage buildings. Along with other humorous gestures, such as lift buttons configured as navels and sheaths of wheat, it also smacks of a quirky, idiosyncratic irreverence that speaks to alternative London's countercultural instincts. But, first and foremost, Coal Drops Yard acts as a metaphor for the strategic ambitions of the wider King's Cross Central scheme; namely to embed the development into the surrounding city by embracing and then imaginatively reinterpreting the character of London (Fig.113).

## McGRATH ROAD, STRATFORD/ LONDON BOROUGH OF NEWHAM

✦ **Architect:** Peter Barber
✦ **Client:** London Borough of Newham
✦ **Type:** Housing
✦ **Completion:** 2019
✦ **Benefit:** Density, Entrances, Grain, Height, Housing, Materials, Paving, Planning, Squares, Streets, Style, Trees, Views

There are not many projects that can combine four key London housing typologies, but in this esoterically charming example of east London new public housing, we find traces of the mews, the townhouse, the council house and, perhaps most surprisingly, the widely historically discredited back-to-back terrace. Architect Peter Barber has been something of a maverick presence on the London housing scene since crafting a number of small, highly contextual residential developments with a strong emphasis on social communality and the contemporary

143

114    McGrath Road channels British and Austrian housing precedents to forge
an enigmatic and virtuoso contribution to London's residential character.

reinterpretation of traditional London housing themes. Back in 2016, with his Worland Gardens row of terraced houses, Barber first patented a distracting feature that has become a recurring presence on much of his residential work since: the parabolic brick arch. It has now reappeared even more enthusiastically on one of his most recent works, a new social housing scheme on McGrath Road between Forest Gate and Stratford.

The scheme provides 26 'tower' townhouses stretched across three or four storeys and arranged around a private residential courtyard. The houses are arranged in back-to-back fashion with properties accessed via their own front door either through the courtyard or directly from the street. Back-to-back houses have a contentious social history in the UK and are often associated with the appalling, insanitary mass housing conditions of the 19th century, when they were rapidly built to accommodate the huge expansion of cities triggered by the Industrial Revolution. After falling out of favour significantly in the next century, they have undergone something of a resurgence of late, with architects such as AHMM at their recent Signal Townhouses scheme in

Greenwich acknowledging back-to-back's ability to achieve high densities within London's fine urban grain. McGrath Road also offers a distinctly more benign reinvention than their discredited 19th century format by providing private roof terraces and generously sized one-, two- and three-bedroomed properties up to 96 sq m (1033 sq ft).

While the back-to-back internal arrangement is not visible from the street, what is clear is the radical form, massing and materiality devised for the building, which provides a variety of inspiring contemporary reaffirmations of London's character. First there is the wonderful brickwork, a pale, chalky, granular stock that immediately alludes to London's traditional stock brick. Next, there is the form of the building, to which the aforesaid signature parabolic arches make such a vivid contribution. The arches are usually extended over two storeys at the foot of each townhouse and enclose its entrance. Together, they form a springing, sweeping arcade that gives the building a strong, civic presence on the street, both powerful and playful at the same time. They also provide an endearingly humanistic touch, like rows of dislodged Dali-esque eyebrows raised in quizzical scrutiny of their surroundings. The positioning of the arched entrances right on the pavement line is another traditional London mews feature and was historically employed on a number of the city's more modest terraces in working-class areas. Here, as on these historic precedents, it gives the terraces a hard, urban edge, one of course relieved by the constant rhythmic leaping of the arches (Fig.114).

This domesticated softening of civic impact, as represented by the playful arches, is another key feature of London's character. This principle is also rigorously conveyed by the array of variously sized windows punched into the walls and by the building's buoyantly inventive massing. The roof, for instance, is sliced into a vivid crenelated skyline of angular turrets and the feature corner of the block is moulded into a smooth, full-height curve. These starkly expressed geometries combine with the heaviness of the solid brick walls to establish a defensive, almost citadel-like feel to the architecture, one that makes some reference to Vienna's legendary 1930 Karl-Marx-Hof social housing but which also has its roots in the muscular, institutionalised formality of early London Peabody and council housing developments, like the Bourne and Pembury estates (Fig.115).

The final London ingredient is the central courtyard. Again, courtyards were a common

feature of London's early social housing and they provide a dynamic expression of the sense of intimacy, enclosure and communality that pervades London's character. Glimpsed and accessed through a single hollow version of the trademark parabolic arches on the street facade, it also provides the voyeuristic urban intrigue of being able to peep into a sheltered, inner private space lurking behind the public street. Although six young trees have been planted in the courtyard, bravely it has been left as a hard-landscaped rather than a soft-landscaped area. In some ways, this is atypical for a city that regularly fills such enclosures with grass and trees. But by combining a residential sense of intimacy and enclosure with the more civic, hard-edged feel of irregular brick arcades and frontages surrounding a private amenity space, it forms a toughened, urbanised and miniaturised version of a typical London square. The courtyard encapsulates a delightful scheme that creatively reinvents key aspects of London's residential character, but does so in an utterly unique manner that brims with playful craftsmanship and quirky, enigmatic whimsy throughout. In keeping with the trailblazing housing tradition that was once embedded into London's municipal fabric, it is all the more impressive for delivering social housing too (Fig.116).

115   Elliptical arches are not only used to frame views but to denote individual residential units.

116   The hard-paved courtyard forms a contemporary version of the communal courtyards that were a common and intimate feature of late 19th- and early 20th-century London council estates.

# NEWPORT STREET GALLERY, VAUXHALL/LONDON BOROUGH OF LAMBETH

✦ **Architect:** Caruso St John

✦ **Client:** Damien Hirst

✦ **Type:** Cultural

✦ **Completion:** 2015

✦ **Benefit:** Alleyways, Art, Grain, Materials, Streets, Views

Architecture constructs streets and then streets construct character. It is the simple reciprocal hierarchy that lies at the very core of our urban condition but one that is rarely given the attention or respect it deserves. In short, in most cases – with tall buildings being a significant exception – streets usually have more of an impact on urban character than individual buildings. But if one such individual building wanted to heighten its urban impact, then adopting the architectural language and convention of the street might just be the way to do it. This is exactly the strategy pursed by architects Caruso St John at their landmark gallery commission for British art's chief provocateur Damien Hirst. One might have expected a zanily avant-garde building in the manner of Hirst's signature formaldehyde pieces. What has been created, however, is a gushing architectural love letter to the street, with the London backstreet in particular being the object of the gallery's affections.

The building lies on an unassuming side street in south London, directly opposite elevated railway arches. It is an innocuous semi-industrial backstreet setting that is replicated thousands of times all across London. The gallery occupies a linked brick terrace of new-build and refurbished blocks that line Newport Street's eastern side. The gallery's central core is a historic one and is formed by a row of three listed Edwardian brick warehouses that were built in 1913 to serve as scenery painting workshops for the nearby West End theatres. These have now been bookended by two new-build brick blocks on either end to form a continuous, uninterrupted brick frontage of five connected volumes. The trio of historic blocks forms the architectural inspiration for the entire composition,

117 Newport Street Gallery carefully crafts a vibrant urban streetscape that strongly resonates with the character of London's backstreets.

118 The elevational treatment skilfully weaves new (*left*) and old (*right*) together.

with its unusual proportions of grouped, low-level windows and high blank walls finding nuanced contemporary echoes on the new facades on either side. A boldly articulated sawtooth roof to the north side and a plainly muscular frontage of punched openings beneath a powerfully projecting upper balcony to the south, both subtly reference the industrial heritage of local roofscape and streetscape while all the while being stealthily attuned to their central historic host (Fig.117).

The result is a wonderfully varied and vivid street frontage, as dramatic and theatrical a piece of urban scenography as the stage sets that were once produced here. The new street frontage happily embraces the fine vertical grain and hectic diversity of form that are key characteristics of London's hidden backstreet hinterlands and are also deeply embedded in the city's urban character. Moreover, the new brick facades cleverly update the Edwardian light industrial language of deep openings, animated roofline, utilitarian form and muscular scale, so that the gallery weaves and stitches old and new together seamlessly to form a compelling exercise in discreet urban needlework. It is important not to take this almost painfully realised subtlety for reticence or timidity, for there is an almost industrial conviction in the manner in which the new building immerses itself so wholeheartedly into the irregularity, irreverence and informality that characterises London's backstreets. In so doing, it marks an assured and empathetic work of contemporary architecture that is so forensically embedded in the rhythmic cadence of the London backstreet that it appears to have been there forever (Fig.118).

## ONE CARTWRIGHT GARDENS, BLOOMSBURY/LONDON BOROUGH OF CAMDEN

- ✦ **Architect:** Maccreanor Lavington (facade)/ TP Bennett
- ✦ **Client:** University Partnership Programme
- ✦ **Type:** Housing
- ✦ **Completion:** 2017
- ✦ **Benefit:** Density, Entrances, Grain, Height, Housing, Materials, Streets, Style

The residential terrace is arguably London's definitive architectural motif. It houses almost a third of London's residents, encloses practically all of its squares, overlooks thousands of its streets and is an essential component of London's urban character. Bloomsbury is a part of London that is intrinsically defined by the terrace. Not only is this evident in its atypical grid plan but also in its remarkable collection of primarily Georgian garden squares. But, for all their beauty, these squares expose one of the limitations of the terrace format as a contemporary housing solution for a large and growing modern city; terraces are low in height and can be relatively low density. While the Victorians were able to stack their terraces up to five or six storeys high in Bayswater and Kensington, Georgian architecture, as applied in Bloomsbury, rarely extends its terraces above three or four storeys. This domesticity is an intrinsic part of Bloomsbury's character and reinforces London's humanist feel, but it will not necessarily help solve London's housing crisis. But what if the residential terrace format could be maintained, and applied to a much larger scale of contemporary building, thereby sustaining London's core character while delivering the significantly higher levels of housing density and supply the city needs? In short, can there such a thing as a contemporary 21st-century London mega-terrace?

The answer is yes, and the proof comes – appropriately enough – in Bloomsbury. One Cartwright Gardens is a student housing block that overlooks landscaped gardens and an elegant early 19th-century Regency crescent, one of Bloomsbury's prodigious contingent of very long terrace ranges of relatively modest height, here four storeys. While the Regency terraces assume the full curvature of the crescent, the new building occupies the entirety of the flat range that faces it. The development provides 1200 student flats and replaces an earlier 1950s housing block of largely undisciplined design. Interestingly and unusually, separate architects were retained for the building itself and the key facade facing the crescent, an admission perhaps of the latter's critical townscape importance. The resultant facade is a barnstorming triumph of monumental moderation. At nine storeys high (plus raised basement) and almost 120 m (394 ft) long, the facade is conceived on a gigantic scale, just a few metres short of the length of Harrods department store and more than twice the height of anything the Georgians conceived on their adjacent terraces. How then does the building relate to its more modest surroundings? The first and most obvious answer is that it is expressed as a terrace. Not a row of houses with individual entrances, but as a monolithic city block with a central entrance flanked on either side by plunging shafts of narrow vertical bays. This is a different kind of terrace to its Georgian precedents, but in massing and proportion it conforms to exactly the same typology (Fig.119).

The brickwork in which the facade is encased also enables it to relate to context. A lusciously pale, buff Danish brick has been selected, its chalky tones and earthy texture relating instantly to the London stock brickwork that is such an intrinsic part of the city's character. And, finally, the facade's masterful elevational articulation is crucial in immersing it into its fabric and helping decompartmentalise a massive facade into smaller, nimbler fragments. Vertically, the facade echoes classical precedents by being divided into a tall rusticated base, a taller middle section and then a shorter top – the latter surmounted by a dormered attic storey. While this maintains the illusion of three horizontal bands, it cleverly conceals the building's multistorey composition: the base, top and attic contain two storeys while the middle contains three. This represents an innovative mutation of classical orthodoxy that the Georgians could never have pulled off, but it still keeps the building firmly within the realms of contextual empathy (Fig.120).

Horizontally, in another familiar classical theme, the facade is divided into bays containing columns of individual windows. But these are no ordinary

bays, they are dramatic, sculpted crevices cut deep into the facade with the attendant recesses expressed as grooved corbels that enclose each bay like a muscular receding hood. This detail is the consequence of the building's innovative prefabricated construction; the facade is formed by a series of precast concrete piers and panels assembled offsite and overlaid with the brickwork finish. The result is that they help lend the facade a powerful sense of depth and three-dimensionality, as if the entire building were sculpted from one gigantic single piece of clay.

While this is certainly no Georgian architectural composition, its inventive contemporary reinterpretation of classical themes is wildly successful. Repetitious but not monotonous, monolithic but not inhuman, this remarkable building falls seamlessly into London's tradition of big civic edifices softened by the subtle introduction of a more intimate, residential character. The block is all the more remarkable because it far exceeds the quality of most of the new student housing being built in London today and also forms one of the most ambitious applications of the emergent, so-called New London Vernacular style to date. This is a style which Maccreanor Lavington, whose expertise with brickwork has crafted many fine London projects, has done much to promote. But, first and foremost, this mighty Selfridges for students offers a powerful 21st-century update of London's terrace typology and usefully demonstrates how it can be applied at bigger scales and densities.

119   One Cartwright Gardens creates a monumental, contemporary version of the traditional London terrace.

120 The monumentality of the terrace is tempered by a clearly defined entrance.

## THE SHARD, LONDON BRIDGE/ LONDON BOROUGH OF SOUTHWARK

- ✦ **Architect:** Renzo Piano
- ✦ **Client:** Sellar Property Group
- ✦ **Type:** Mixed-use
- ✦ **Completion:** 2012
- ✦ **Benefit:** Height, Materials, Names, Squares, Transport, Uses, Views

During the hotly contested public inquiry held into Renzo Piano's proposed London Bridge skyscraper in 2003, a barrister acting for the then English Heritage[30] (opposing the proposals) claimed that, were the building ever built, it would be like 'piercing a shard of glass into the historic heart of London'.[31] The developers won, and the name stuck. As the tallest building in Western Europe, the

Shard clearly subscribes to the high-rise typology that has inflicted terrible harm on London (Fig.121). And even today, several years after its completion, it continues to divide opinion, with some decrying the social inequality inherent in the £50 million price tag for some of its flats and others making unkind (and unfounded) architectural comparisons with North Korea's monstrous Ryugyong Hotel in Pyongyang.

With such a fractious backstory, why then would the Shard make it onto a shortlist of recent buildings that have enhanced London's character? It does so for three principal reasons: its usage, its public realm impact and, most importantly, its form. The Shard bills itself as Europe's first 'vertical city', which means that, as well as offering the offices that are in many ways the obligatory function of the tall-building model, it also incorporates a hotel, a number of bars and restaurants, a retail arcade, a public rooftop viewing gallery and flats, albeit preposterously expensive ones. In so doing, the Shard's functional variety and committed public access help to humanise a building type previously

121 At 310 m (1017 feet) high, the Shard is the tallest building in Western Europe.

overwhelmingly associated with corporate monoculture and residential exclusivity. By turning the conventional private rituals of an office block into the civic events of a semi-public building, the Shard successfully engages with the humanistic patterns of openness, accessibility and diversity on which London's character is based.

The Shard has also had a significant and largely positive impact on the public realm of the surrounding area. For centuries, Southwark has been the poor southern relation to the wealthy City of London on the north side of the Thames, a place whose ancient reputation for vice and debauchery was reflected in an urban fabric historically characterised by deprivation and underdevelopment. While the rejuvenation of Bankside from the late 1990s meant that much of this legacy was already being transformed, long before the Shard came into being, the skyscraper inevitably acted as a catalyst for a renewed regeneration drive. Accordingly, it helped galvanise the redevelopment of London Bridge train and bus station at its base, and the visual theatricality of seeing the Shard almost float upwards from the

122 Despite its height, the Shard embeds itself into the character of London by evoking the familiar traditional form of a supersized church spire.

glass roof of the station's rebuilt upper concourse forms a dramatic and thrilling juxtaposition of public and private realm. Equally, the onset of the Shard compelled the National Health Service to complete an external cosmetic makeover of the ghastly Guy's Hospital Tower next to it, a small act of mercy, if nothing else. And even better, the Shard's very existence necessitated the demolition of the Southwark Towers office block, a 1970s high-rise eyesore that had blighted the area for decades. Of course, this being London, regeneration is a double-edged sword and the Shard has now opened the floodgates to all manner of inappropriate and historically insensitive proposals. But even with such corrosive caveats, the Shard set new benchmarks for how private development can bequeath public improvement (Fig.122).

But the biggest and most successful means by which the Shard enhances London's character is found in its form. Piano spoke of being heavily influenced by Canaletto's famous mid-18th-century paintings of London from the Thames which depicted the dome of St Paul's Cathedral surrounded by a constellation of church steeples. The narrow pyramidal form of the Shard therefore is partially inspired by the outline of one of these steeples, a giant, secular 21st-century spire sheathed in steel and glass rather than lead and stone. In so doing, the Shard reaches deep into London's architectural backstory to seize upon a form of architecture that subliminally resonates with the heritage and populace of the city. Steeples in London are as familiar a part of London's historic fabric as canals in Amsterdam and, by harnessing one as the partial conceptual inspiration for a new building, Piano has cleverly maintained the Shard's contemporary credibility while simultaneously allowing it to become a symbolic and poetic expression of London's historic fabric and urban heritage (Fig.123).

The fractured humility of the Shard's extraordinary summit also helps in this regard. Many London tall buildings are utterly clueless about how to compose their crowns, and mishaps range from the superfluous angular toupee hurled onto Salesforce Tower to the inflamed tumescence of the Walkie Talkie. The Shard takes a more subtle approach and, by expressing its summit as an open, fragile and almost incomplete cage delicately

123   The form of the Shard was partially inspired by the constellation of church steeples that Canaletto depicted surrounding St Paul's in the 1740s.

enclosed within jagged fragments of glass and steel, the building attains a gentle, poignant transparency that quite literally allows the city to flow through it rather than it imposing itself on the city. It is the same humble but highly effective townscape trick that Wren used on the open baroque lanterns of his church spires and it denotes a thematic synchronicity which once again embeds the Shard into London's architectural heritage. The Shard also uses low-ion glazing which, depending on light conditions, either variously enables the entire structure to appear almost transparent or, on the cloudy rainy days that are such a common feature of London weather, forms a glistening glacial mirror which reflects the city back onto itself. In a city that has struggled for decades to consolidate tall buildings within its historic fabric and whose character has suffered so much as a result, the Renaissance subtext of the Shard's form and the haunting frailty of its summit prove that design can be an effective mediator between heritage and height (Fig.124).

124   In a contextual concession that most of London's skyscrapers ignore, the Shard's summit emphasises fragile transparency rather than overbearing belligerence.

151

# Appendix

Table 2 London Public Space Character Matrix

| | | Civic | Residential | Adapted from Residential | Commercial/ Retail | Privately Developed | Soft Landscape Centre |
|---|---|---|---|---|---|---|---|
| 1 | Arnold Circus | | ● | | | | ● |
| 2 | Bank Junction | ● | | | | | |
| 3 | Bedford Square | | ● | | | ● | ● |
| 4 | Belgrave Square | | ● | | | ● | ● |
| 5 | Berkeley Square | | ● | | ● | ● | ● |
| 6 | Bloomsbury Square | | ● | | ● | ● | ● |
| 7 | Broadgate Circle | ● | | | ● | ● | |
| 8 | Buckingham Palace Rond Point | ● | | | | | |
| 9 | Cabot Square | | | | ● | ● | |
| 10 | Cadogan Square | | ● | | | ● | ● |
| 11 | Canada Square | | | | ● | ● | ● |
| 12 | Cavendish Square | | ● | | ● | ● | ● |
| 13 | Charterhouse Square | | ● | | | ● | ● |
| 14 | Chester Square | | ● | | | ● | ● |
| 15 | Covent Garden Piazza | ● | | ● | ● | ● | |
| 16 | Duke of York Square | | | | ● | ● | |
| 17 | Eaton Square | | ● | | | ● | ● |
| 18 | Exchange Square | | | | ● | ● | |
| 19 | Finsbury Avenue Square | | | | ● | ● | |
| 20 | Finsbury Circus | ● | | ● | | | ● |
| 21 | Finsbury Square | | | ● | ● | ● | ● |
| 22 | Fitzroy Square | | ● | | | ● | ● |
| 23 | Golden Square | | ● | | ● | ● | ● |
| 24 | Gordon Square | | ● | | | ● | ● |
| 25 | Granary Square | ● | | | | ● | |
| 26 | Grosvenor Square | | ● | | | ● | ● |
| 27 | Guildhall Yard | ● | | | | | |
| 28 | Hanover Square | | | ● | ● | ● | ● |

| Hard Landscape Centre | Carriageway Centre | Irregular/ Informal Composition | Regular/ Formal Composition | Fully Pedestrianised | Part- Pedestrianised | Dominant Focal Centrepiece | Fountains |
|---|---|---|---|---|---|---|---|
|  |  |  | ● |  |  | ● |  |
| ● | ● | ● |  |  | ● |  |  |
|  |  |  | ● |  |  |  |  |
|  |  |  | ● |  |  |  |  |
|  |  | ● |  |  |  |  |  |
|  |  |  | ● |  |  |  |  |
| ● |  |  | ● | ● |  |  |  |
| ● |  |  | ● |  | ● | ● | ● |
| ● |  | ● |  |  | ● | ● | ● |
|  |  | ● |  |  |  |  |  |
|  |  | ● |  |  | ● |  |  |
|  |  |  | ● |  |  |  |  |
|  |  | ● |  |  |  |  |  |
|  |  | ● |  |  |  |  |  |
| ● |  |  | ● | ● |  | ● |  |
| ● |  | ● |  | ● |  |  | ● |
|  |  |  | ● |  |  |  |  |
| ● |  | ● |  | ● |  |  |  |
| ● |  | ● |  | ● |  |  |  |
|  |  |  | ● |  |  |  |  |
|  |  | ● |  |  |  |  |  |
|  |  |  | ● |  | ● |  |  |
|  |  | ● |  |  |  |  |  |
|  |  | ● |  |  |  |  |  |
| ● |  |  | ● | ● |  | ● | ● |
|  |  |  | ● |  | ● |  |  |
| ● |  | ● |  | ● |  |  |  |
|  |  | ● |  |  |  |  |  |

| | | Civic | Residential | Adapted from Residential | Commercial/ Retail | Privately Developed | Soft Landscape Centre |
|---|---|---|---|---|---|---|---|
| 29 | Hans Place | | ● | | | ● | ● |
| 30 | Horse Guards Parade | ● | | | | | |
| 31 | Hyde Park Corner | ● | | | | | ● |
| 32 | Kensington Square | | ● | | | ● | ● |
| 33 | King's Cross Square | ● | | | | | |
| 34 | Leicester Square | ● | | ● | ● | ● | ● |
| 35 | Lincoln's Inn Fields | | ● | | | ● | ● |
| 36 | Lowndes Square | | ● | | | ● | ● |
| 37 | Manchester Square | | ● | | | ● | ● |
| 38 | Montgomery Square | | | | ● | ● | |
| 39 | New Street Square | | | | ● | ● | |
| 40 | Oxford Circus | | | | ● | | |
| 41 | Park Crescent | | ● | | | | ● |
| 42 | Parliament Square | ● | | | | | ● |
| 43 | Paternoster Square | ● | | | ● | ● | |
| 44 | Pelham Crescent | | ● | | | ● | |
| 45 | Piccadilly Circus | ● | | | | | |
| 46 | Portman Square | | ● | | ● | ● | ● |
| 47 | Royal Crescent | | ● | | | ● | ● |
| 48 | Russell Square | | ● | | ● | ● | ● |
| 49 | St James's Square | | ● | | ● | ● | ● |
| 50 | Sloane Square | ● | | ● | ● | ● | |
| 51 | Smlth Square | | ● | | | ● | |
| 52 | Soho Square | | ● | | ● | ● | ● |
| 53 | Tavistock Square | | ● | | | ● | ● |
| 54 | Trafalgar Square | ● | | | | | |
| 55 | Trinity Church Square | | ● | | | ● | ● |
| 56 | Vincent Square | | ● | | | ● | ● |
| 57 | Waterloo Place | ● | | | | | |
| 58 | Westferry Circus | | | | ● | ● | ● |
| 59 | Westminster Cathedral Piazza | ● | | | | | |
| 60 | Wilton Crescent | | ● | | | ● | ● |
| | | 30% | 51% | 10% | 40% | 75% | 62% |

| Hard Landscape Centre | Carriageway Centre | Irregular/ Informal Composition | Regular/ Formal Composition | Fully Pedestrianised | Part- Pedestrianised | Dominant Focal Centrepiece | Fountains |
|---|---|---|---|---|---|---|---|
|  |  | • |  |  |  |  |  |
| • |  | • |  | • |  |  |  |
| • |  | • |  |  |  | • |  |
|  |  | • |  |  |  |  |  |
| • |  | • |  | • |  |  |  |
|  |  | • |  | • |  | • | • |
|  |  | • |  |  |  |  |  |
|  |  | • |  |  |  |  |  |
| • |  | • |  | • |  |  |  |
| • |  | • |  | • |  |  |  |
| • | • |  | • |  |  | • |  |
|  |  |  | • |  |  |  |  |
|  |  | • |  |  |  |  |  |
| • |  | • |  | • |  | • |  |
| • |  |  | • |  |  |  |  |
| • |  | • |  |  | • | • | • |
|  |  | • |  |  |  |  |  |
|  |  |  | • |  |  |  |  |
|  |  | • |  |  |  |  | • |
|  |  | • |  |  |  |  |  |
| • |  | • |  |  |  |  | • |
| • |  | • |  |  |  | • |  |
|  |  | • |  |  |  | • |  |
|  |  |  | • |  |  |  |  |
| • |  |  | • |  | • | • | • |
|  |  |  | • |  |  | • |  |
|  |  | • |  |  |  |  |  |
|  | • |  | • |  | • | • |  |
|  |  |  | • |  |  |  |  |
| • |  | • |  | • |  |  |  |
|  |  |  | • |  |  |  |  |
| 38% | 5% | 62% | 38% | 23% | 15% | 25% | 15% |

155

# Notes

1    Peter Ackroyd, *London: The Biography*, Chatto & Windus, London, 2000.

2    Steen Eiler Rasmussen, *London: The Unique City*, Penguin Books, Harmondsworth, 1934.

3    ibid.

4    Judith Hook, *The Baroque Age in England*, Thames & Hudson, London 1976.

5    See www.trustforlondon.org.uk.

6    Nikolaus Pevsner, *London 1: The Cities of London and Westminster*, Buildings of England, 12, Penguin Books, Harmondsworth, 1957.

7    New London Architecture, *London Tall Buildings Survey*, 2019.

8    New London Architecture, *London Tall Buildings Survey*, 2018.

9    Historic Royal Palaces planning objection letter to City of London director of Built Environment, 17 December 2018.

10    Jonathan Leake, 'Oxford Street worst in the world for diesel pollution', *Sunday Times*, 6 July 2014.

11    François Truffaut, *Hitchcock*, Simon & Schuster, New York, 1966.

12    New London Architecture, *London Tall Buildings Survey*, 2018.

13    Greater London Authority, *Housing in London*, 2018, at https://data.london.gov.uk/blog/housing-in-london-2018-report/.

14    Land Registry UK House Price Index, at http://landregistry.data.gov.uk/app/ukhpi, accessed April 2017.

15    NYC Real Estate, Marketproof Inc, at https://marketproof.com.

16    Office for National Statistics, Census Data for England and Wales 2011, at www.ons.gov.uk/census/2011census.

17    HM Land Registry, Price Paid Data, 2015, at http://landregistry.data.gov.uk/app/ppd.

18    Andrew Carter and Paul Swinney, 'The UK's rapid return to city centre living', 22 June 2018, at www.bbc.co.uk/news/uk-44482291.

19    'Boeing 747', in *Building Sights*, series 3, BBC television series, transmitted 15 January 1991.

20    Greenspace Information for Greater London (2015) states that 33 per cent of London's land is allocated to public green space. See www.gigl.org.uk/keyfigures/.

21    See www.worldcitiescultureforum.com/assets/others/181108_WCCR_2018_Low_Res.pdf.

22    Peter Smithson and Alison M. Smithson, *Italian Thoughts*, n.p., 1993.

23    *The Global Attractions Attendance Report*, AECOM, Themed Entertainment Association (2017). See www.aecom.com/wp-content/uploads/2019/05/Theme-Index-2018-4.pdf.

24    London Assembly, *Creative Tensions: Optimising the Benefits of Culture through Regeneration*, 2017.

25    See www.westminstertransportation services.co.uk/projects/project_details.php?id=210; BNP Paribas Real Estate, *Pan-European Footfall Analysis*, 2017.

26    Commission for the Built Environment submission to 20 Fenchurch Street public inquiry, 5 March 2007.

27    Birmingham City Council, *Birmingham Big City Plan*, masterplan report, 2011.

28    Deirdre Hipwell, 'Broadgate revamp wins go ahead but must face one last hurdle', *The Times*, 20 April 2011.

29    Jonathan Glancey, 'One New Change: never brown in town', *The Guardian*, 20 October 2010.

30    English Heritage still exists today as a charity charged with the preservation of historic buildings. However, the statutory government quango role English Heritage previously occupied is now held by Historic England.

31    See www.shardldn.com/construction-history-html/.

# Index

Note: **bold** page numbers indicate figures; *italic* page numbers indicate tables.

1 City Road (Lewis, 1929) 128, **128**
1 Poultry (Stirling) 128, 135, 136
1 Princes Street (1929) **50**
5 Broadgate (Make, 2015) 119–21, **120**
7 Lothbury, City of London (1866) **54**
20 Fenchurch Street *see* Walkie Talkie
  tower
22 Bishopsgate, City of London (PLP,
  2020) 26–7, **118**, 123–5, **124**, **125**
22 Hanover Square 29, 84, *152–3*
30 St Mary Axe (Foster) 101, 121
33–35 Eastcheap, City of London
  (Roumieu, 1868) 99, 137
60 Queen Victoria Street (Foggo
  Associates, 2000) 135–7, **135**, **136**

Abramovitz, Max 36
Ackroyd, Peter 8
Admiralty Arch (Webb, 1912) **72**, 110, 111
AHMM (architects) 67, **67**, 144
Aldwych 11, 23, 63, 92, 105, 127–8
Alexandra Road Estate (Brown) 20, 100
Alsop, Will 31
Altes Museum, Berlin (Shinkel, 1823–30)
  34, **34**, 35
*Angel's Wings* (Heatherwick) **47**
Archway Gyratory 32, 76
Arnold Circus 87–8, *152–3*
Arup Associates 87, **87**, 119, 129–30

Baily, Edward 47
Bank of England (1791) **50**
Bank Junction 71, 82, *152–3*
Bankside 114, 150
Barber, Peter 69, 143
Barbican Centre (Chamberlin, Powell &
  Bon, 1965–82) 37–8, **37**, 54, 100
Barbican Centre for Music (Diller
  Scofidio + Renfro) 32
Barcelona (Spain) 21, 52, *53*, 61, 92, 104
Barry, Edward Middleton 39
Barton Street, Westminster (1722) **19**
Battersea 54, 129
Bayswater 50, 53, 147
Beck, Harry 103
Bedford Square 76, 86, **86**, 105, *152–3*
Belgrave Square 86, 87, *152–3*

Belgravia 50, 53, 73, 86, 87, 93, 95, 98,
  105, 107, 132, 133, 139
Bennetts Associates 88
Benson & Forsyth (architects) 131, 132
Berkeley Square 84, *152–3*
Berlin (Germany) 11, 34, **34**
Bernini, Gian Lorenzo 40, 41, 46
Big Ben 69, 108, 112
Birmingham (UK) *53*, 69, 116, 119, 124
Bishop's Court, City of London **47**, 139
Bishopsgate, City of London **28**, **65**,
  **118**, 126
Bishopsgate Goodsyard 30, 126
Bloomburg Building, City of London
  (Foster) 61, 74, 101, 135, 136
Bloomsbury 11, 12, 23, 35–6, 50, 63, 98,
  105, 106, 147
Bloomsbury Square 86, *152–3*
Boundary Estate, Shoreditch 19, 30, 88
Bourne Estate, Clerkenwell 68, 145
Bramante, Donato 40
British Museum 34, 35–6, **35**, 95, 101, 106,
  **106**, 139
Broadgate 30, 88, 119–21
Broadgate Circle (Arup Associates, 1987)
  87, **87**, 88, 120, *152–3*
Broadway Malyan (architects) 130
Brown, Neave 20, 100
Buckingham Palace **20**, 21, 47, 49, 55, 61,
  70, 71, 110, 111, **133**
Buckingham Palace Road Point 82, 83,
  *152–3*
BuckleyGrayYeoman (architects) 46, 135
Burnham, Daniel **110**

Cabot Square, Canary Wharf 88, *152–3*
Cadogan Estate, Chelsea 17, 50
Cadogan Square 84, *152–3*
Camden 11, 12, 80, **81**
Camden Courtyards, Kentish Town
  (Sheppard Robson) 52, **53**
Camden High Street **81**, 96
Canada Square, Canary Wharf 88, *152–3*
Canary Wharf **15**, 16, 17, 23, 54, 64, 72,
  82, 88, 98, 107, 116, 119, 129
Carlton House Terrace (Nash, 1832) **94**, 110
Carnaby Street 60, 94

Caruso St John (architects) 146
Cavendish Square 86, *152–3*
Central St Giles (Piano) 50, 72
Chamberlin, Powell & Bon 37–8, **37**
Chambers, William 36
Chapter Spitalfields, Tower Hamlets (TP
  Bennett, 2010) 119, 125–7, **126**
Charing Cross 75
Charles II 13, 18, 61, 95
Charterhouse Square 84, *152–3*
Chelsea 11, 50, 52, 73, 76, 81, 82
Chester Square 84, *152–3*
Chichester Rents, Camden/City of
  London (ORMS, 2017) 46, 135, 137–9,
  **137**, **138**
City of London 7, 11, **14**, **22**, **25**, 27, 32,
  45, 46, 47, **47**, 50, **54**, **58**, **59**, 61, 64,
  72–3, 74, 75, 79, 89, 98, 100, 102, 107,
  109, 135–7, 138
City of London Magistrates Court
  (Whichcord, 1873) 135
Clements Lane, City of London **22**
Coal Drops Yard, King Cross Central
  (Heatherwick Studio) 142–3, 143
Conran, Terence 17
Copenhagen (Denmark) 48, 49, 66
Corner, James 57–8
Covent Garden 11, 20, 23, 45, 46, **60**, 64,
  75, 107, 108, 139, 142
Covent Garden Piazza 82, 83, 84, *152–3*
Crutched Friars 74, **74**

de Blasio, Bill 27
Diller Scofidio + Renfro 32
Dixon Jones 39, 56, **56**, 76, **76**
Downing Street 94, 95, 108
Drapers Hall, City of London (1772) **54**
Duke of York Square 76, 88, *152–3*

Ealing 11, 64, 81
East End 16, 19, 88, 108, 116, 126
Eaton Square 86, *152–3*
Eccleston Yards, Victoria/Westminster
  (BuckleyGrayYeoman, 1028) 46, 135,
  139–41, **140**, **141**
Economist Building, St James's
  (Smithson) 105

Elephant and Castle  32, 68
Embankment  105, 114
Eros statue, Piccadilly Circus  46–7, 55
Euston Road  33, 58, 89, 93, 105
Exchange Square  88, *152–3*
Exhibition Road  32, 76, **76**

Finsbury  11, 67
Finsbury Avenue Square  88, *152–3*
Finsbury Circus  87, *152–3*
Finsbury Square  88, *152–3*
Fitzrovia  50, 63
Fitzroy Square  76, 86, *152–3*
Fleet Street, City of London  27, 42, **58**, **78**, 89, 100, 111, 113, 137
Floral Court, Covent Garden (Kohn Pedersen Fox)  46
Foggo, Peter  119, 135, 136
Foreign Office (Scott, 1860)  21, **21**
Foster, Norman  100–101, 103, **106**, 127, 135, 139
French Ordinary Court, City of London  46, 75

Garnier, Jean-Louis Charles  38
Gehry, Frank  100
George IV  13, **15**, 61, 87
Gherkin (Foster)  101, 121
GMW Architects  72, 135
Golden Square  19, 84, 85, *152–3*
Goldfinger, Erno  100
Gordon Square  84, *152–3*
Gower Street  **67**, 93
Granary Square  32, **56**, 57, **69**, 76, 82, 83, 142, *152–3*
Greenwich  11, 23, 75, 91, 93
Grenfell Tower  68–9
Grosvenor Square  86, 87, *152–3*
Guildhall Yard  82, *152–3*
Guinness Trust  19–20, 30

Hackney  11, 19, 53–4, 107, 115
Hadid, Zaha  80, 100
Hampstead  12, 63, 66, 68, 101
Hanover Square  29, 84, *152–3*
Hans Place  84, *154–5*
Harrison, Wallace K.  36
Hasilwood House (Mewes and Davis, 1926)  **28**
Haussmann, Georges-Eugène  17, 38, 61, 90, 93, 98
Hawksmoor, Nicholas  106
Heatherwick, Thomas/Heatherwick Studio  **47**, 103, **103**, 141, 142, **143**
Hepworth, Barbara  47
Hirst, Damien  146
Hitchcock, Alfred  49

Hoe Street, Leyton  **96**
Hopton's Almshouses (1749)  **28**
Horse Guards Parade  69, 76, 82, *154–5*
Howard Fairburn and Partners  49
Hyde Park  47, 56, 64, 74, 76, 108
Hyde Park Corner  30, 33, 82, *154–5*

Inns of Court  13, 108–9, 137
Isle of Dogs  114, 116

Jacobs, Jane  36
John Lewis department store, Oxford Street  47
Johnson, Philip  36

Kapoor, Anish  47
Kensington  11, 12, 52, 57, 80, 81, 82, 87, 96, 147
Kensington Square  84, *154–5*
Kentish Town  **53**
King Street, Covent Garden  **60**
King's Cross Central  **115**, 129, 135, 139, 141–3, **142**, **143**
King's Cross Square  32, **70**, 82, *154–5*
King's Reach, Westminster  112, 114
Kingsway  17, 23, 63, 92, 105, 111, 127
Kohn Pedersen Fox (architects)  139

Lambeth  11, 93, 146–7
Lamb's Conduit Street  74, 75
Landseer, Edwin  46
Lasdun, Denys  100
Le Sueur, Hubert  75
Leadenhall Building (Rogers)  26–7, 100, 121, 124
Leadenhall Market  73, 97, **97**, 98
Leicester Square  19, 57, 82, 105, *154–5*
Levitt Bernstein (architects)  67
Lewis, William  **128**
Leyton  **96**
Lincoln Center, New York (Johnson/ Harrison/Abramovitz/Saarinen, 1959–66)  36–7, **36**
Lincoln's Inn Fields  20, **48**, 84, 85, *154–5*
Lipton, Stuart  125
Little Venice  116, **116**
Lloyds Building (Rogers, 1986)  100, **100**
Loampit Vale  75
Lombard Street  79, **80**, 89, 121, **122**
London Bridge  107, 114
London Underground  81, 100, 103
London Wall  33, 105
Los Angeles (US)  52, **53**, 66
Lovat Lane, City of London  **25**, 46, **46**, **102**, 121
Lowndes Square  84, *154–5*
Lubetkin, Berthold  20

Ludgate Hill  11, 42, 102, 111
Lutyens, Edwin  21, 55

Maccreanor Lavington (architects)  68, 126, 147, 148
McGrath Road, Stratford/Newham (Barber, 2019)  135, 143–5, **144**, **145**
Make Architects  119, 139
Mall, the  17, 23, 63, 76, 92, 105, 110, 111
Man in Moon Passage  74, **74**
Manchester Square  84, *154–5*
Martin, Leslie  32
Marylebone  **12**, 23, 61–3, 96
Mayfair  7, 11, 46, 60, 66, 75, 86, 95, 98, 104, 107, 129
ME London Hotel (Foster + Partners, 2013)  119, 127–9, **127**
Metropolitan Opera House, New York  36
Michelangelo  40
Millbank Tower (1963)  27, 64
Millennium Dome (Rogers)  100
Minster Court, City of London (GMW Architects)  135
Mitterrand, François  17
Montgomery Square, Canary Wharf  88, *154–5*
Monument (Wren, 1677)  16, 47
More London (2003)  **17**, 57, 114
Motcomb Street  94, **95**
Muswell Hill  67, 101

Napoleon III  38, 61, 93, **94**
Nash, John  13, 35, 61, 71, 73, 87, **87**, 91, **94**
Natural History Museum  72, 107
Nelson's Column (Baily)  47, 66, 71
Neo Bankside (2014)  **28**
New Street Square  88, *154–5*
New York (US)  6, 11, 27, 36–7, **36**, 52, **53**, 57, 61, **61**, 63, 66, 79–80, 81, 92, 103, 104, 124
Newport Street Gallery, Vauxhall/Lambeth (Caruso St John, 2015)  135, 146–7, **146**
Nine Elms  30, 119, 129–31, **130**
Northumberland Avenue  92, 105
Notting Hill  51, 73
Notting Hill Gate  32, 104
Nouvel, Jean  100, 133, 134
Nova Victoria (PLP/Benson & Forsyth, 2016)  30, 61, 74, 119, 131–3, **132**, **133**

O'Donnell + Tuomey  **71**
Old Royal Naval College (1669)  **15**, 23
One Cartwright Gardens, Bloomsbury/ Camden (Maccreanor Lavington/TP Bennett)  126, 135, 147–8, **148**, **149**
One New Change (Nouvel, 2010)  **10**, 79, 119, 133–4, **134**
One Pancras Square (Chipperfield)  142

Oxford Circus 87, 88, *154–5*
Oxford Street 47, 49, 89, 92, 100, 105, 109, **110**
Oxo Tower, South Bank 80

Palais Garnier (Garnier, 1861–75) 38–9, **38**
Palestra Building (Alsop) 31
Pantechnicon, Belgravia 95, **95**
Paris (France) 6, 11, 13, 17, 24, 38–9, **38**, 49, 52, *53*, 60, 61, **61**, 66, 69, 82, 90, 92, 93, **94**, 98, 103, 114
Park Crescent (Nash, 1821) 87, **87**, *154–5*
Park Lane 33, 92, 93, 105, 108
Parliament Square 17–18, 32–3, **33**, 58, 69, 82, 104, 105, 110, *154–5*
Paternoster Square 17, 82, *154–5*
Paul Davis + Partners 88
Peabody Trust 19–20, 30, 145
Pelham Crescent 87, *154–5*
Pevsner, Nikolaus 21
Piano, Renzo 50, 72, 79, 100, 109, 149, 150
Piccadilly 64, 96
Piccadilly Circus 47, 55, 56, 79–80, 87, 88, *154–5*
Pimlico 73, 87, 132, 133
PLP (architects) 123, 131
Pool of London 114, 115
Port of London 114, 116
Portland House, Victoria (Howard Fairburn & Partners) 49, 64, 131–2
Portman Square 84, *154–5*
Portobello Road **51**
Primrose Hill 50–51, **51**, 73, 101
PRP architects 71

Queen Elizabeth Olympic Park 47, 57–8, **58**, 98, 108, 111
Queen Victoria Memorial, Buckingham Palace 55, 110

Rasmussen, Steen Eiler 8, 16
Regent Street 61, 64, 70, 71, 91, **91**, 94, 98, 109
Regent's Canal 116, **116**
Regent's Park **18**, 50, 56, 61, 73, 93, 98
Rogers, Richard 100, **100**, 136
Rolfe Judd (architects) 130
Rome (Italy) 11, 23, 40–41, **40**, 46, 98
Romney Road, Greenwich 90, 91
Roumieu, R.L. 137
Royal Albert Hall 47, 72, 102, **102**, 107
Royal Courts of Justice 95, 99
Royal Crescent 87, *154–5*
Royal Festival Hall (Martin) 32, 107
Royal Opera House (Barry/Dixon Jones, 1857–8/1990–99) 39–40, **39**, 95
Russell Square 57, 84, *154–5*

Saarinen, Eero 36
St Edmund, King and Martyr Church (City of London) **22**
St George Wharf Tower (Broadway Malyan) 27, 32, 64, 130
St James's Market 76, 139
St James's Park 18, **20**, 21, 70, 102, **104**, 111–12, 113
St James's Square 84, 85, **85**, *154–5*
St James's Street 90, 91
St Michael's Alley, City of London **45, 59**
St Pancras Station 71, 73, 99, 141
St Paul's Cathedral (Wren, 1710) **10, 23**, 25, 26, 27, 41–2, **41**, 66, 71, **78, 99**, 102, 109, 111, 112, **112**, 113, 133
St Peter's Basilica, Rome (Bramante/ Michelangelo/Bernini, 1506–1626) 40–41, **40**
Saw Swee Hock LSE Student Centre (O'Donnell + Tuomey, 2014) **71**
Schinkel, Karl Friedrich 34, **34**
Scott, Giles Gilbert 21, 103
Selfridges department store (Burnham, 1909) **110**
Seymour Place, Marylebone **12**
Shad Thames 94, 115
Shard (Piano, 2012) **46**, 109, 121, 124, 135, 149–51, **149, 150, 151**
Shepherd Market, Mayfair 46, 73
Shepherd's Bush 75
Sheppard Robson **31**, 52
Shoreditch 11, 47, **77**, 87–8, 107, 108
Signal Townhouses, Greenwich (AHMM, 2017) 67, **67**
Sloane Square 82, *154–5*
Smirke, Robert/Smirke, Sydney 35
Smith Square 84, *154–5*
Smithson, Peter 105
Soho 72, 75, 79, 98, 107
Soho Square 19, 84, 85, *154–5*
Somerset House 36, 56, **56**, 71, 105, 114
South Bank 57, 70, 80, 107, 114
South Kensington *53*, 73, 76, 107, 142
Southwark 11, **28**, 31, 77, 99, 150
Spitalfields 12, 47, 126
Stanton Williams Architects 40, 141, 142
Stirling, James 128, 135
Strand 89, **90**, 95, 98, 127

Tavistock Square 86, *154–5*
Thames, River 6, 11, **44**, 102, 105, 113–15
Thatcher, Margaret 17
Threadneedle Street 75
Throgmorton Street, City of London **14**, 60, 99
Tower Bridge 72, 99, 102, 113, 114

Tower Hamlets 19, 125–7
Tower of London 26, **26**, 71, 100, 102, 114
TP Bennett (architects) 125, 147
Trafalgar Square 32, 35, 46, 47, 55, **55**, 71, 75, 76, 82, 83, **83**, 84, 102, 105, 110, *154–5*
Transport for London 18, 32, 103–4
Trinity Church Square 86, *154–5*

Vauxhall 54, 130
Via Triumphalis (George IV/Nash) 13, **15**, 61, 87
Victoria 46, 49, 52, 74, 131–3, 139
Victoria and Albert Museum 57, 72, 107
Victoria Embankment (1869) 57, **57**, 92
Victoria Square 132, **132**
Vienna (Austria) 13, 23, 82, 145
Vincent Square 84, *154–5*
Viñoly, Rafael 100, 121

Walkie Talkie tower (20 Fenchurch Street, Viñoly, 2014) 6, **25**, 27, 31, 64, 78, 89, 119, 121–3, **122, 123**, 150
Walthamstow 11, 97, 115
Waterloo Bridge 112, 114
Waterloo Place **15**, 63, 82, 83–4, 102, 110, *154–5*
Webb, Aston **72**
Wembley Stadium 111
West End 19, 21, 50, 54, **54**, 64, 88, 93, 107, 109
Westferry Circus 87, *154–5*
Westminster 11, 18, 27, 28, 52, 77–8, 80–81, 98, 108, 112
Westminster Abbey 70, 78, 99, 108, 109, 112
Westminster Cathedral 71, 100, 109
Westminster Cathedral Piazza 82, *154–5*
Westminster, Palace of 25, 69, 71, 73, 78, 99, 108, 113, 114
Whichcord, John Jr 135
Whitehall 21, 69, 71, 90–91, 94, 98, 105, 108, 112
WilkinsonEyre (architects) 40, 141, 142, **143**
Wilton Crescent 87, *154–5*
*Winged Figure* (Hepworth) 47
Wood Green 11, 63–4
Woolwich 11, 75, 114
Woolwich Central (Sheppard Robson, 2014) 30, 31, **31**
Worland Gardens (Barber, 2016) 69, 144
Wren, Christopher 13, 18, 47, 58, 61, 95, 96, **99**, 109, 151
*see also* St Paul's Cathedral

# Illustration Credits

The reproduction of the illustrations listed below (by figure number) is courtesy of the following copyright holders:

Ajepbah 23

Beata May 34
Bernard Gagnon 69

Carcharoth (Commons) 12
Colin/Wikimedia Commons 17, 124
CVB 66, 72

David Iliff 35, 64, 75, 80, 82, 83
Diego Delso 56

Eluveitie 102

Gareth E. Kegg 58
Gary Houston 76
Guillaume 5

Hufton+Crow, courtesy of Stanton Williams 54

Ike Ijeh 2, 4, 7, 8, 14, 15, 16, 18, 19, 20, 21, 22, 24, 26,
    29, 30, 31, 32, 33, 36, 39, 40, 44, 45, 46, 47, 49,
    50, 55, 57, 60, 61, 62, 68, 73, 74, 77, 85, 86, 89,
    90, 91, 92, 93, 94, 95, 96, 97, 98, 99, 100, 101,
    103, 104, 105, 117, 118, 122

John Sturrock 87, 111, 112, 113
John Sturrock, courtesy of Stanton Williams 42,
    53

Kingmiwok 43

Marc Cluet 121
Marcus Peel 106, 107, 108
Matt Chisnall 109, 110
Morley von Sternberg 114, 115, 116

Paul Riddle 59
Peter Rivera 27
Philippe Cendron 65

Robert Mintzes 25

Sberla 11
Simeon87 84
Simon Kennedy 38
Spudgun67 67
Stephen Richards 13

Tim Crocker 119, 120
Tim Soar, courtesy of AHMM 52
Tom Page 9

Umezo Kamata 71
Uwe Aranas 88

WebDesign.com 48
Wei-Te Wong 6

Yair Haklai 28